PRAISE FOR

MARRIAGE
TRIGGERS

"'But how do we stop fighting?' A question we, as marriage mentors, are often asked. Guy and Amber Lia have an answer! With a refreshing transparent and biblical approach, *Marriage Triggers* is an amazing resource to help you discover practical ways to exchange anger for kindness and conflict for peace. This book will help you and your spouse discover: you're not alone in your struggle, how to resolve conflict without shouting, ways to re-establish friendship in marriage, hope for real happiness—and so much more! Well done Guy and Amber. In a world desperate for answers, I pray your biblically sound message transforms marriages to joyfully reflect God's love, joy, hope, and peace."

—RHONDA STOPPE, "No Regrets Woman," author of
six books, including *The Marriage Mentor:
Becoming the Couple You Long to Be*

"From the day we published *Triggers* for parents, Amber and I have received hundreds, if not thousands, of requests from husbands and wives asking for this book! How wonderful that the Lias took up the challenge! Together, they offer biblical insight into our marriages' most common triggers and give us practical application so that we might learn to respond with gentleness and love rather than bitterness and strife. Even if you don't struggle with big, explosive anger, recognizing these common triggers will safeguard your marriage and help you grow in your communication skills as husband and wife. Truly. If you knew that your marriage could be transformed through the reading of this book, wouldn't you do it? Well, it can! So grab a copy of the book and grab your spouse today."

—WENDY SPEAKE, co-author with Amber Lia of *Triggers* and *Parenting Scripts*, and author of *The 40-Day Sugar Fast*

"*Marriage Triggers* is a must-have resource for any couple who desires a thriving marriage. With a well-balanced approach, Guy and Amber give your marriage a fighting chance by addressing triggers that threaten to divide you. Confront angry patterns with grace-infused conversations as you move toward a healthier, hope-filled relationship."

—ADAM REID, lead pastor at Central Church and KATIE M. REID, author of *Made Like Martha* and co-hosts of the live marriage show *Stop! Hammock Time*

"Marriage is rarely what we expect, but it is good because God says it is good. So how do we protect what is precious in God's eyes? Leaving no stone unturned, Guy and Amber dive deep into the common issues that plague couples everywhere. Their transparency and practical advice is a breath of fresh air. *Marriage Triggers* reminds us we aren't alone and gives us the courage to fight for the marriage we've always dreamed of. And the one God wants for us."

—PATRICK and RUTH SCHWENK, founders of TheBetterLifeMinistry.com, and authors of *For Better or for Kids* and *Faith Forward Family Devotional*

"Whether your marriage is on the brink of a major crisis or not, this book is for you! Amber and Guy offer practical and biblical advice for dealing with common triggers we all face in marriage. Take the time to invest in your marriage—you won't regret it!"

—KATIE, Shelby, MI

"It has been an exciting journey to read this book together as spouses. It helped us to recognize triggers and face them with a biblical view. The insights and vulnerability that Guy and Amber shared has been an inspiration for us to get into deeper conversations. Helping us to remember we are not fighting against each other but together for our marriage."

—PIETER and MARIALE, Evergem, Belgium

"After reading this book, I realized that this is the perfect gift for newlyweds! It sounds strange, but even though couples often go through premarital counseling before tying the knot, there usually is very little preparation for what the couple will actually face as the months turn in to years and decades. How amazing would it have been to have received this book when we first got married?! *Marriage Triggers* could literally equip a couple for marital success since it outlines the primary triggers and responses most couples deal with and then gently provides biblical guidance on how to avoid the deep-rooted patterns of anger, bitterness, isolation, idols and self-focus!"

—CASSIE, San Tan Valley, AZ

"This is not a one-time read! *Marriage Triggers* is a must-have tool for every engaged and married couple. It establishes the biblical truth and framework for the marriage Christ desires us to thrive in."

—GLORIA and JOE, Bartlett, IL

"I recently read Chapter 8, 'When Your Life Looks Different Than You Thought It Would,' and it was timely for me. This chapter is one of the things that God has used to challenge my perspective and remind me to appreciate what I have been blessed with and submit to God's plans. It helps remind me of what matters the most in life, which is Christ and people, and the people part starts with family."

—LON, Detroit, MI

"*Triggers: Exchanging Parents' Angry Reactions for Gentle Biblical Responses* CHANGED the way that I parent my children, so naturally when I heard about *Marriage Triggers* I jumped in with both feet! Per usual, Amber Lia does not disappoint. Even better, this time we get the male perspective from her husband, Guy! Their authenticity, vulnerability, and love for Jesus come together in this fantastic new book that is absolutely chock-full of biblical truths. *Marriage Triggers* opened up so many wonderful opportunities for my husband and I to reconnect and to have honest, open conversations about our relationship. God is present in the pages of this book and thanks to His work through the Lias, God is present in our marriage again too."

—NATALIE, Lexington, KY

"This book has been so convicting and encouraging. My marriage will never look the same! Thank you, Guy and Amber, for being open about your own triggers and passionate about helping others grow toward the true purpose of marriage!"

—ERIN, Winfield, PA

"Having read and loved *Parenting Triggers*, I was so excited to learn that Amber was working on *Marriage Triggers*. *Marriage Triggers* is equal parts grace, conviction, and fun. It is so easy to read and each chapter has practical things for me to implement in my marriage straightaway. Each chapter I feel challenged, but not so much that I am despairing—Amber and Guy help me to realize that I am not alone in my struggles and there is a way to move forward in my marriage."

—ANNA, Sydney, Australia

"*Marriage Triggers* is a wonderful balance of conviction and encouragement, wrapped up beautifully with God's word. Whether your marriage is in need of a minor tune-up or a major overhaul, this book is a great tool that will help you to see those annoying marriage triggers as opportunities to draw closer to Jesus."

—JESSICA, Southmayd, TX

"*Marriage Triggers* allowed us to stop and focus on each other, our marriage, and turn our hearts to God as we show love and grace to each other. We aren't done, but I feel that *Marriage Triggers* set us on a new healthy path. I can't recommend the book enough!"

—MARK, Ventura, CA

MARRIAGE
TRIGGERS

EXCHANGING SPOUSES' ANGRY REACTIONS
FOR GENTLE BIBLICAL RESPONSES

AMBER LIA & GUY LIA

HOWARD BOOKS

ATRIA

New York   London   Toronto   Sydney   New Delhi

HOWARD BOOKS

ATRIA

An Imprint of Simon & Schuster, Inc.
1230 Avenue of the Americas
New York, NY 10020

First Howard Books trade paperback edition January 2020

HOWARD BOOKS/ATRIA BOOKS and colophon are
trademarks of Simon & Schuster, Inc.

For information about special discounts for bulk purchases, please contact Simon
& Schuster Special Sales at 1-866-506-1949 or business@simonandschuster.com.

The Simon & Schuster Speakers Bureau can bring authors to your live event. For
more information or to book an event, contact the Simon & Schuster Speakers
Bureau at 1-866-248-3049 or visit our website at www.simonspeakers.com.

Manufactured in the United States of America

1 3 5 7 9 10 8 6 4 2

Library of Congress Cataloging-in-Publication Data has been applied for.

ISBN 978-1-9821-2791-6
ISBN 978-1-9821-2792-3 (ebook)

Marriage Triggers is dedicated to the husbands and wives who are desperate for hope and longing for change. We have prayed over you for many years, and our expectation is that the Holy Spirit will enable you to exchange your angry reactions for gentle biblical responses. May you and your spouse experience every good thing that God prepared for your marriage and may your hearts be filled with the love of Christ toward one another as you embrace His love for you, His Bride.

TABLE OF CONTENTS

TABLE OF CONTENTS

SECTION TWO:
INTERNAL TRIGGERS

FOREWORD

*I*n our family, we love going to the beach, but the beach doesn't seem to love us back. We pay a heavy price to strip down into our swimsuits, because we're all prone to getting sunburned. Apparently Ancestry.com was correct and our Irish roots run deep on both sides of the family and for our kids too! Our pasty white complexion is just part of being in the Willis family, but we don't let that deter us from having some fun in the sun. We pack extra aloe and sunblock, but despite our best efforts, we all know we're going to be driving home with blistered backs and sensitive, red skin.

Even after a great day of fun and waves, when someone pats us on the back afterward it evokes a visceral reaction. The seemingly harmless back pat hits such a sensitive area of sunburn that we often overreact with a scream. We've seen our boys push each other, and even come close to throwing punches after being touched on their sunburned skin.

When we're touched in a place of pain, vulnerability, insecurity, or sensitivity, it can create unintended pain and uncontrolled outbursts. Our family's reaction to sunburns is, in essence, a trigger. A trigger isn't usually as visibly apparent as a sunburn. Triggers are usually hard to see. They're more likely to live within the mind and heart than the skin. Still, these invisible, emotional "sunburns" can trigger powerful and painful responses when left unchecked.

In our work with married couples, we've found that most couples are wandering through a minefield of triggers in their marriage. The triggers can be anything from sexual issues to financial issues to in-law stresses to past hurts to a myriad of other factors. Most couples don't have the tools to properly identify these triggers and then develop a proactive game plan to deal with them in a healthy way.

We are strongly convinced that properly dealing with triggers is one of the biggest factors that leads to a healthy marriage. This is why we are thrilled that Guy and Amber Lia have written this book on the triggers in your marriage. The book you're about to read has the power to transform your marriage and your life if you'll takes its lessons to heart. Seriously.

I know that probably sounds like we're overselling it, but we're not! Imagine what your marriage could be if you were completely in tune with each other's greatest struggles, needs, desires, and hurts. Imagine how much closer you could be as husband and wife if those topics that cause instant arguments could become the very topics that lead to your most meaningful conversations. Imagine being the safest place on earth for each other. Those are the very things that will happen if you'll apply the lessons you're about to read in this book.

Guy and Amber Lia have given a profound gift to every married couple on earth by writing *Marriage Triggers*. It's a modern masterpiece of marriage ministry because they had the courage to be so vulnerable and honest in sharing their own story. As the reader, you're about to experience the full spectrum of human emotion through the true stories and timeless biblical truths on the pages to come. You're going to laugh, possibly cry, have new thoughts you've never considered, and have your eyes opened to the depth of intimacy, wholeness, and healing that God desires for your marriage.

Take these lessons to heart. Put them into practice. We believe your marriage will be forever transformed as a result.

—Dave and Ashley Willis, authors of
The Naked Marriage and hosts of *The Naked Marriage* podcast

INTRODUCTION (AMBER)

I'm convinced that more marriages are triggered than not. Couples feel angry and frustrated by all the things that set them off—things like finances, lack of trust, intimacy in the bedroom, personality differences, and busy schedules. Readers often ask me if their anger is justified and how to know the difference. It's an important question for us to examine before we look into these thirty-one chapters that lie ahead. Author Lou Priolo, in his book *The Heart of Anger*, writes this insightful truth about righteous and unrighteous anger:

> "If your anger is due to your recognition that a holy God
> has been offended by another's behavior, that anger is righ-
> teous . . . On the other hand, if your anger is the result of not
> having your personal desires met, that anger is usually sinful.
> In other words, if we are angry because someone (without
> sinning) prevented us from having what we really wanted,
> our anger is sinful. Of course, it is possible (even probable in
> those situations where another person's sin against God is

also an offense to us) to have both righteous anger and sinful anger residing in our hearts at the same time."[1]

This really is the idea of hating the sin but loving the sinner, isn't it? We should feel righteous indignation when we see sin and evil in the world, or in the lives of our spouses. But what should really get our backs up is that sin is an affront to the God we love, not because it's an affront to us personally. Being impacted by our spouse's sin doesn't give us the right to indulge in our own.

Husbands and wives all over the world are waking to a new day and as soon as it registers mentally that they are awake, the gloom of their strained relationship fills their hearts. We want our marriages to be better, but instead, our triggers often leave us bitter—or broken. Many of us go to bed angry, even though we may be familiar with Ephesians 4:26–27 (ESV):

"Be angry and do not sin; do not let the sun go down on your anger, and give no opportunity to the devil."

The anger we sometimes feel can be overwhelming. It was for me. When you read chapter 1, you will see what I mean. Everyday triggers are often the culprit. The "little things" we don't know how to address—or have been addressing wrongly—make us angry and frustrated, with little hope for change. If you have wondered how to break out of the cycle of reactionary outbursts, cold shoulders, resentment, and pain that harms your relationship, you are not alone. There is a better way! And it's not as hard as you think.

Being impacted by our spouse's sin doesn't give us the right to indulge in our own.

This book walks you through thirty-one of the most common marital issues that sabotage great relationships, like poor communication, lack of spiritual leadership, busy schedules, and different parenting styles. The truth is, our unrighteous anger can quickly lead to other sinful attitudes and actions. But it doesn't have to. If you are like me and my husband as we face our own triggers in marriage, each new day brings with it two options:

Carry on with the same conflicts and frustrations, **reacting angrily** and fanning the flames until everyone gets burned,

or

Learn to practice **responding biblically** so that love can reign in our hearts, strengthening our own personal walks with God, and resulting in a blessed marriage.

For many years now, I have been walking through a variety of triggers and gentle biblical responses with parents as they navigate the changing stages and dynamics of parenting. Almost as soon as *Triggers: Exchanging Parents' Angry Reactions for Gentle Biblical Responses* was hot off the press, the Holy Spirit planted the seed in my heart to write *Marriage Triggers*. In my first book in this series, written with my co-author, Wendy Speake, we heard from hundreds of parents who read and reread our book. Often, they expressed this "aha" moment:

Triggers was not helping them fix their kids so they wouldn't have to be angry anymore. *Triggers* was showing them, trigger by trigger, and verse by Bible verse, that peaceful parenting was not about changing their kids, but about changing their own attitudes and reactions to the triggers in their parenting. The result was a strengthened faith and a radically transformed home.

Marriage Triggers is no different. These thirty-one common triggers in marriage are the result of hundreds of responses and several years of feedback from husbands and wives who feel angry in their relationships. Guy and I spent too many years angry with one another, ourselves. *We get it.* We have learned firsthand, and heard from the lips of hundreds of couples, that anger doesn't always look like throwing dishes and screaming voices. It can be cold or hot. Bitter or sweetly manipulative. Withdrawn or aggressive. Vengeful or hopeless. Careless or clingy. Indifferent or idolatrous. Loud or quiet. Passionate or passive. But every sinful reaction has one thing in common: it's a foothold for all kinds of nastiness. A stepping-stone that leads us away from the happy marriage that God desires us to have with one another.

As you read, you aren't getting the doctoral treatise from two PhDs who have studied healthy relationships. Nor are you getting an intellectual examination of triggers and how to avoid them. You are getting the transparent and practical insights from a couple, a lot like you, who love God and are still learning to love one another well. We are walking right beside you, writing from a place of need for our own marriage. And you'll get a look at differing perspectives. You'll see (Amber) or (Guy) next to each chapter title to indicate which of us is addressing each marriage trigger. We anticipate that like so many men and women, you, too, may be struggling with your emotions, feeling hopeless, or wondering if things will ever change. God offers all of us this promise:

"And we know that in all things God works for the good of those who love him, who have been called according to his purpose." (Romans 8:28, NIV)

Can our triggers work for good?

Can our responses lead to a better marriage?

Can our anger lead us to a more purposeful relationship?

We believe they can, because we believe God.

Guy and I encourage you to identify *trigger moments* as much as you identify the triggers themselves. Having conversations about conflicts late at night when you are tired, in the car where you feel confined, or in the heat of the moment as emotions run rampant is less than ideal and usually leads to even more anger and frustration. Once you have identified your "trigger moments," put a plan in place to regularly come together outside of conflict to lovingly discuss triggers when they arise.

Some of our friends have agreements in place with their spouses to never start conversations regarding their marriage triggers during their identified trigger moments. As a result, they are able to talk with one another without anger fueling the conversations, and harmony has been restored in their conflict resolution. When you are faced with a marriage trigger, say something like, "Honey, there is something on my mind that I'd like to talk through with you. Can we set a time on Wednesday to talk about it together?" Sometimes it's hard to delay these conversations, but exercising self-control is a great first step toward being the peacemakers God asks us to be.

Let's not waste another moment living angered. The book you have in your hands is not a formula, full of cut-and-dried tips and tricks for a happy life, but if you are willing to let the Holy Spirit open your heart to transformation, you will surely experience the goodness of God in your marriage. Read prayerfully and with great expectations for what God can do. Whether you are reading alone or with your spouse, your marriage is about to segue from triggered to triumphant.

SECTION ONE:

EXTERNAL TRIGGERS

When the things that trigger us toward anger have everything to do with them . . .

Sometimes, our triggers toward anger and frustration catch us by surprise. We walk into the living room and find a mess, or our car needs unexpected repairs, or our bank account takes a hit. Whether we are triggered by a lack of spiritual leadership, busy with overwhelming schedules, or feeling the pressures of the workplace, the triggers we discuss in this first section are some of the most common everyday moments that tempt us toward unrighteous anger.

CHAPTER 1

WHEN YOU MARRIED MR. WRONG OR MS. ALL WRONG (AMBER)

Our wedding day was picture perfect. Ten bridesmaids, ten groomsmen, and two hundred of our closest friends and family. We spent the better part of a year planning every detail. My friends and I labored for hours, handcrafting tiny flowers for our invitations. My wedding dress was the most beautiful gown I had ever seen, and my fiancé, Guy, had arranged for my favorite childhood car, a restored MG, to be our "getaway" car after the ceremony. Three of the dearest men alive were ready to speak during the ceremony. Our bags were packed for a relaxing and romantic honeymoon in Playa del Carmen. Every detail was perfect.

Little did I know that in the midst of all our wedding perfection, there were one—*or two*—major flaws: the bride and groom. Guy and I knew that marriage was not warm fuzzies all the time. We'd witnessed for ourselves plenty of marriages that ended in disaster. The statistics were pretty harsh, and we took them seriously.

Even so, those early days as newlyweds were challenging. Many couples experience a "honeymoon phase" for a good long while. Ours ended only a few months into our marriage. It was a rude awakening from the fairy-tale dreams I imagined and the happy home life Guy desired. *We were triggered from the start.* Guy couldn't live up to my expectations. He reacted in frustration, which fanned my hurt feelings into my own angry reactions. My sinful indignation justified his sinful words or actions and there we were, looking up at an unattainable cloud nine from the slippery pit of misery.

The things that formed a wedge between us were both internal and external triggers—ranging from long work hours to personal childhood wounds, issues with intimacy and connectedness, clashing schedules, financial differences, and eventually, differing parenting styles. No amount of premarital counseling or good intentions prepared us for the real deal. What Guy and I were experiencing wasn't unusual. We were the norm. For many years now, I have worked with thousands of families who seek to navigate away from angry parenting toward more gentle and biblical responses. As a result, I have been privy to how many of these same triggers threaten not only unified parenting, but marriage itself in many of our homes. Instead of feeling ashamed for the angry feelings and reactions we often display toward our spouses, we can have hope that there is a better way. *A gentle biblical way.* And it's within the grasp of every husband and wife who longs for change.

On our wedding day, we had no idea that our vows would be tested so soon. We wrote them with the heartfelt emotion and wonder of two young pups in love, but we said it loud and clear for everyone to hear as part of our pledge to one another: "I will not divorce you." We took divorce off the table on day one, not aware of how we would be tested in this commitment. God knew we would need the reminder. He knew we needed to say it out loud in front of those two hundred guests. He knew we would be faced with the truth that love is often a choice.

It sounds a little callous. A little *cold*. This idea that love is a decision you choose to make, rather than an emotion or a feeling. A commitment to honor your vows and to honor God. I recently heard a pastor speak on "The Defense of Romantic Love in Marriage." And he was right. God intended marriage to be a beautiful picture of love—both in its choices and in its emotions. But what happens when you marry Mr. Wrong? Because I did. And sadly, he married Ms. All Wrong. You see, it boils down to the purpose of life. Jesus summed it up for us when the religious leaders of His day asked Him this question:

"Teacher, which is the greatest commandment in the Law?" Jesus replied: "'Love the Lord your God with all your heart and with all your soul and with all your mind.' This is the first and greatest commandment. And the second is like it: 'Love your neighbor as yourself.'" (Matthew 22:33–39, NIV)

There it is. What do you do when you marry the "wrong" man or woman? You love God and you love your spouse as well as you love yourself. We could never fulfill that kind of love outside of a radical, devoted, passionate love for God. And we sure can't love like that if we're busy meditating on all the ways our spouses fall short. You see, every man is the wrong man. Every woman is the wrong woman. Satan set out to mar paradise in the garden with Adam and Eve, and they took the bait by taking the bite. And no one ever loved unconditionally again.

No man can love to the point of dying for his enemies on the cross. Only Jesus. For a long time, I wanted my husband to be Mr. Right who knew me better than anyone, could read my mind, showered me with words of affirmation, and came home with flowers every week. I wanted him to pick the right size shirt when he bought me a gift and set me up behind a white picket fence. But that wasn't my Guy. My Guy was who God made him to be. He's the guy who is so devoted that I never question his loyalty. He's the guy who wrestles with his sons on the floor, and wrestles for their hearts in prayer. He's the guy who shows courage as he follows his God-sized dreams and faithfully takes risks when it would be easier to play it safe. He's the guy who loves me better than anyone ever has. Imperfect, yes, but loving me the best he knows how. I almost missed it. I almost missed all that love because it didn't look the same way I pictured it in my dreams or movie-made expectations.

I know God tells husbands to love their wives as Christ loved the church. But the moment I start trying to be my husband's conscience and remind him of that because I don't think he is doting on me enough, speaking my love language, prioritizing the way I do, leading like I want him to, or being Mr. Right in whatever capacity that looks like, then I am focusing on the wrong thing. And our marriage will suffer for it.

How about you? Do you wonder what it would be like if your wife would just . . . ? Or if your husband would finally . . . ? Are there times when you question whether marrying your spouse was the wrong decision? Imagining the "what if" scenarios traps us in our negativity. These mental gymnastics leave our emotions twisted and our thinking contorted. Meditating on such questions can do us no good. Our spouses can't compete with the unspoken ideals of a mental match game. The apostle Paul wrote to the early Christians, testifying that his own desire to live life to the full necessitated leaving the past in the past, and striving to make the future worthy of his desire to become more like Christ. I believe we can apply this to our marriages too:

"... But one thing I do: forgetting what lies behind and straining forward to what lies ahead, I press on toward the goal for the prize of the upward call of God in Christ Jesus." (Philippians 3:13–14, ESV)

Let's settle the matter, here in the first chapter. The moment you said "I do" to your wife or husband, your marriage became a match made in Heaven. We won't encourage you to bury your emotions or ignore the challenges of the past that may now be affecting your everyday lives, but only when revisiting the past serves to bring healing and propel us forward is it a good use of our time and mental energy. If those thoughts cause you anger, angst, and agony, and if they *Our spouses can't compete with the unspoken ideals of a mental match game.* harm your relationship, leave them in the dust as you, like Paul, press on toward the prize of spiritual growth and marital harmony. Recognize that every one of us is flawed and has room for improvement. Be open to what God may have for you, *not your spouse*, as you spend the next thirty-one days reading through *Marriage Triggers.*

I married Mr. Wrong. He got Ms. All Wrong. *But it's alright.*

It's alright because we know that no man or woman is perfect. It's alright because we are both sinners saved by amazing grace. It's alright because we choose to love when the other is unlovely. And it's alright because when we fail at that, we wake up to a new day and new mercies (Lamentations 3:22–23). I can spend my time grieving what I don't have. Or I can spend time worshiping a God who loves me unconditionally and sent His only Son

The moment you said "I do" to your wife or husband, your marriage became a match made in Heaven.

to die for me on the cross. I can bemoan that my husband doesn't love me like that and wallow in guilt about my own self-centeredness. Or I can rejoice that God's love for us is perfect and honor Him by focusing on the way my husband loves me.

Spend your energy on loving God and loving others. Start with your spouse. Don't do it because you want a result. Do it because your life is not your own, but was bought with a precious price, and realize the love you seek is already yours in the person of Jesus Christ. Our spouses were never meant to be our Savior or the source of our happiness.

I suspect you married Mr. Wrong and that you may well be Ms. All Wrong. But I pray that today you see that *it's alright.*

Let's Pray: "Dear God, thank You for designing marriage to be a picture of Your love for me. I know that You want my husband/wife and me to experience marriage as You designed it to be. I'm tired of longing for what I don't have. Help me to see my spouse as You see him/her. Work in my heart, Lord! Satisfy me in ways only You can do. Fix my eyes on You and every time I begin to meditate on negative thoughts about what my husband/wife may be doing wrong, fill me with humility, forgiveness, and hope. Remind me that we are not perfect; we are forgiven. Then help us to love one another as You do, Lord. Let love rule our hearts and minds. In Jesus' Name, Amen!"

CHAPTER 2

WHEN THE HOUSE IS A MESS (AMBER)

*I*n my first *Triggers* book, my co-author, Wendy Speake, says that when your house is a mess, "don't let it make a mess out of you." Unfortunately, the clutter and chaos of a home in disorder impacts both husbands and wives in negative ways. Many couples feel defeated by the state of their homes, but there are both practical and biblical responses for this trigger that can make a big difference.

Some of us got the shock of our lives when we moved in together after the wedding and discovered how slovenly our bride or groom had become seemingly overnight. We hear from just as many husbands as wives about the messiness of their homes. At the risk of being stereotypical, women can't seem to figure out why men dump their clothes on the floor instead of the laundry hamper and men can't figure out why the house looks like a tornado hit it the day after being cleaned. It may seem like a small matter on the surface, but the tensions that build when a home is no longer a haven can chip away at our happiness. And worse, if we give in to our angry impulses, the defeated feelings of failure to keep a house clean and the lack of understanding for one another's responsibilities construct walls around our hearts.

Guy and I recognize that plenty of couples reading this book have not started families or are empty nesters, and the insights we will offer in this chapter will be fitting for you too, but one of the top triggers we deal with is among couples with children in the home. When kids come into the picture, keeping the house orderly and clean is a massive challenge. I read a meme on Instagram the other day that said this: "And then one day we decided we were tired of sleeping in and doing whatever we wanted whenever we wanted in a clean house, and so we had kids."[2] If this weren't so true, it'd be funny.

When I was single, everything in my house had its place. The moment our oldest son was born, I was as bewildered as my husband when the house went from clean to cluttered in no time at all. The addition of "all the things" necessary for a baby crowds space in the house and the car. Laundry loads multiply faster than we can keep up. At Oliver's three-month well baby checkup, the pediatrician gave me a sympathetic smile and said, "I'm betting his reflux is creating a lot of extra laundry for you, isn't it?" I burst into tears. Someone understood how overwhelmed I felt!

Of course, babies themselves require attention 24/7. The time we spent cleaning our homes or doing other necessary household maintenance before kids entered the picture shifts to the demands of parenting. We aren't prepared for it. Infants seem small, but they require big amounts of our time and energy. As families grow, so do all the needs, clothing to launder, dishes to wash, and messes to clean. The older kids get, the more room they take up and the more "stuff" we acquire.

Family management is often a learned skill that takes some

tweaking to implement once kids get old enough to help. It's also not everyone's strength, so attempting to keep everyone and everything orderly may be even more challenging for certain personalities. Meanwhile, our longing for a clean space is frustrating. As soon as we clear a space, debris finds its way back in no time at all. I often feel like I never get ahead of the housework, and I know I'm not alone.

A few years into our marriage, Guy was laid off from his job. Until he got a taste for what it was really like being home with three young children, he couldn't appreciate how hard it was to keep up with cleaning our home and looking after the kids. Once he saw the challenge, he quickly got on board, partnering with me in significant ways to divide the labor. It has made all the difference! I almost never wash a dish. He leaves most of the laundry up to me. Neither of us ever leaves something for someone else. In our marriage, if we see a need, we fill a need. Instead of "huffing and puffing" as you walk into a room and see the cluttered countertops, jump in with an attitude willing to serve. I must admit, Guy is better about jumping in on tasks than I am. When I see him stepping up to help me even though he has had a long workday, my love and respect for him grows tremendously.

> *In our marriage, if we see a need, we fill a need.*

Jesus showed His love through serving others. If we say we love our spouses but don't serve them, our definition of love is not biblical. This also means that if you are not willingly serving your spouse, he or she may not be feeling loved. Your own actions may very well be hindering your ability to both give and receive affection.

You may be realizing by now that *Marriage Triggers* is not

about triggers in and of themselves. Nor is it a rule book for changing your spouse. But if we can learn to examine our own hearts and the way we relate to our spouses, we may also discover how much we love one another.

For Guy and me, becoming a team that valued one another was a gradual process that required we lay down our preconceived notions of our roles (more on that in chapter 13), trading them for a servant's heart that simply tries to do what is best in the moment to help one another. Even though we both work and have demands outside the home, we now view our marriage as a team effort, working toward a common goal of keeping our house clean and organized, together. Your specific situation may look different from ours, but don't settle for the same old way of doing things. If it's not working, do something different! *Think something different.* Invite the Holy Spirit in to help you problem-solve. But more than anything, exchange your exasperation for empathy and humility so that when you see a need, your first response is to fill that need.

> *Jesus showed His love through serving others. If we say we love our spouses but don't serve them, our definition of love is not biblical.*

Besides the practical side of becoming a team regarding housework, cleaning up the house has as much to do with cleaning up our attitudes as it does with a mop or broom. Wives, guard your heart against resentment for how little your husband may help you. Communicate outside of conflict, when you can kindly paint a picture of your need for him to be more involved with the kids and around the house. Be specific and reasonable about what you ask from him. *But do ask.* Women tend to do all the things and then harbor resentment—which really isn't fair if we aren't communicating our needs. If we are going to feel like martyrs, let it be for something that really merits martyrdom, not because we feel alone in our household tasks.

Husbands, be open to considering that your wife is doing her best and that the job is 24/7. Consider that there may be more than meets the eye that she is up against to keep the house clean and organized. Be willing to look for opportunities to show her you are her partner in every way, stepping in to do things you may not have considered before. Take the time to acknowledge all the things that go unacknowledged daily. It means the world to me when my husband stops to say, "Honey, thanks for always doing the grocery shopping for our family." I'd be fine without hearing him say that to me, but the fact that he does creates a positive environment and communicates to me that he pays attention to me and appreciates me. How often are you in the habit of doing the same? Looking for ways to breathe life into our spouses is preventive medicine for triggers. When we seek out ways to serve and bless our spouses, we grow in humility and godly character, but we also combat triggers before they become triggers in the first place. Being proactive in our marriages prevents us from being reactive in our marriages.

Mark 10:45 (ESV) says, "For even the Son of Man came not to be served but to serve, and to give his life as a ransom for many." This verse is a good litmus test for our attitudes when it comes to housework. Imagine if your spouse embodied this attitude. How might your perspective change if you meditated on Jesus' example as you picked up dirty socks for the hundredth time in the span of a day? God will probably never ask us to give up our lives on a cross. Are we willing to give them up to make smaller sacrifices in the service of our spouses? Are we willing to lay aside

Being proactive in our marriages prevents us from being reactive in our marriages.

judgment of our husband or wife if the china hutch doesn't pass the white-glove test for dust? Might we be willing to trade a Saturday of golfing to rearrange the garage for our wife? Could we stop procrastinating about cleaning the rugs when we know our husband has asked us to do so?

One of my favorite Scriptures is Colossians 3. In verses 12–14 (ESV), we find a life-changing attitude on display:

"Put on then, as God's chosen ones, holy and beloved, compassionate hearts, kindness, humility, meekness, and patience, bearing with one another and, if one has a complaint against another, forgiving each other; as the Lord has forgiven you, so you also must forgive. And above all these put on love, which binds everything together in perfect harmony."

And later, in verse 23: "Whatever you do, work heartily, as for the Lord and not for men."

Remember, triggers are *opportunities* for growth. If you tend to be messy, this trigger is an opportunity for you to improve in this department, working "heartily as for the Lord." If you have had a poor or critical attitude about your spouse's approach or lack thereof to housekeeping, this

God will probably never ask us to give up our lives on a cross. Are we willing to give them up to make smaller sacrifices in the service of our spouses?

is your opportunity to check your attitude, "bearing with one another" and speaking lovingly about this issue with your spouse. Your wife may not win the award for best housekeeper. It may be true that your husband is clueless when it comes to helping around the house. And yet, the Bible never encourages us to point fingers in a haughty or angry manner. Instead, God asks us to have compassionate hearts. To be kind. God urges us to be humble, meek, and patient. He wouldn't tell us to "bear with one another" if we wouldn't often find ourselves in circumstances where that was necessary.

Whatever we do, we are to "work heartily, as for the Lord and not for men." Being more concerned with pleasing an audience of One, both in our work ethic and our attitudes toward our spouses when they fall short, is foundational in helping us overcome this conflict. Some of us may have allowed our need for a tidy home to become more important than our spouse's need to be treated lovingly. A clean house brings with it a sense of harmony that is temporary. Tomorrow will come and so will its messes. Serving from a place of humility and choosing to love our spouses and honor God brings a peace and tranquility that lasts.

Let's Pray: "Dear Lord, we don't want to give in to the trigger of having a messy house. I feel angry and frustrated over the condition of our home and I don't want to feel that way . . . Lord, please intervene on my behalf. Remove the conflict and hurt feelings so we can work toward a solution together. Help us to view the other person through compassionate and loving eyes. Lord, ultimately, I want to honor You with everything I do and say. Let me grow in humility and love for my spouse and help us so that we no longer resort to anger or yelling over our home. Give us creative ideas to help us with the mess, give us wisdom to let go of what we cannot change, and guard our hearts so that our attitudes and actions demonstrate love and grace. In Jesus' Name, Amen!"

CHAPTER 3

WHEN YOU ARE MARRIED TO A BACKSEAT DRIVER (GUY)

*A*backseat driver is a passenger in a vehicle who is not controlling the vehicle but who excessively comments on the driver's actions and decisions to control the vehicle. Sound familiar? If this is a trigger in your marriage, it can be dealt with in a way that preserves your relationship and makes the journey enjoyable instead of fraught with tension and strife.

This one hits close to home. I confess, I have a problem with my wife's habit of backseat driving. When she pipes up from the passenger seat, it triggers me immediately. I must come clean, though: The few times she opted to drive with me sitting in that awkward passenger seat, I have become the backseat driver myself! Worse yet, sometimes I do it to get back at her! Terrible, I know. That's not the gentle biblical way to handle backseat drivers.

Early on in our dating days, we were driving home from a late-night movie. It had been drizzling a few hours before, so the roads were a bit wet, but traffic was light. Amber and I were talking about the movie and having a good time connecting. I am sure I was trying to look super cool, with my elbow up on the window, my right hand at twelve o'clock on the steering wheel so she could see my powerful arms flex while driving. Out of nowhere, a driver came from behind me in the next lane on the right, cutting me off. I swerved from one lane to the other, narrowly missing another car. Once we were back in our lane, safe and sound, Amber laid into me about being more careful and keeping in my lane. "What if there had been another car next to us!" she stammered. I was caught off guard. I thought, "Wait, I just saved you from a terrible accident! It wasn't my fault!" I know she was startled, scared, and surprised, but being a single guy, I wasn't used to receiving criticism for, well, pretty much anything—especially when I felt I had done an excellent job of protecting my date!

Thankfully, Amber married me, swervy lane maneuvers and all. We have had many conversations about driving and the reasons we both fall into the habit of backseat driving. We recognize that this tendency stems from a lack of control and a desire to feel safe. I had to admit that I often ride the warning bumps in between lanes, and while I never thought it was a big deal, it immediately causes stress to mount in Amber's body. Recognizing that and being willing to change my ways is a loving thing to do as her husband. Amber has learned that not everything I do while driving is putting her and our children in peril. She has learned to have faith in my excellent driving record and to calmly communicate with me when I'm at the wheel. Instead of screeching, "Watch out!" she has practiced saying things like, "Honey, would you mind backing off the car's bumper in front of you? It's making me uncomfortable." Even if I know that the distance between me and the car in front of me is adequate, it's no big deal for me to say, "Sure, Honey," and then follow through so that she can relax. I don't need to argue and defend myself, because she is more important than my pride.

Romans 12:16 (NASB) is a helpful verse when we consider ways to bless our spouses on the road:

"Be of the same mind toward one another; do not be haughty in mind, but associate with the lowly. Do not be wise in your own estimation."

Whether you are the backseat driver or the one who is triggered by your spouse's need to tell you what to do, putting on the mind of Christ is essential for a peaceful ride. Humility considers what the other person is saying and is open to correction. Humility isn't concerned with its own way and does not jump to unnecessary conclusions—as if an accident is imminent. If you are the passenger, work on *being the passenger.* If you are the driver, *work on your driving.* Even just taking one another's feelings to heart and making small steps toward a more peaceful ride is a godly response to triggers on the road. Instead of being a backseat driver, make your impulsive interjections take a backseat to gentler ways of communicating.

Like many of the triggers we discuss in this book, it comes down to making active decisions to love, trust, think the best about each other, and bless each other with our responses to concerns that are raised. Because I do 95 percent of the driving in our family, I feel strongly that this is mostly an issue that I take responsibility for, and I bear the burden of self-improvement in order to take that stress away from my wife. I battle my pride in this issue

> *If you are the passenger, work on being the passenger. If you are the driver, work on your driving.*

every time, but it is a great area of growth for me, and I committed to it because I love my wife.

Instead of being a backseat driver, make your impulsive interjections take a backseat to gentler ways of communicating.

Still, sometimes my ego gets in the way. At those times, I recognize that pride is at play. It's a tough sin to contend with for both men and women alike, and there are many verses in the Bible that address this contentious quality.

Proverbs 16:18 (NIV): "Pride goes before destruction, a haughty spirit before a fall."

Proverbs 11:2 (NIV): "When pride comes, then comes disgrace, but with humility comes wisdom."

But perhaps the most fitting verse for those of us triggered by backseat driving is found in Proverbs 13:10 (NIV): "Where there is strife, there is pride, but wisdom is found in those who take advice."

Practically, there are some things that couples can put in place to help alleviate this trigger. Keep in mind, you backseat drivers, that your interjections aren't just frustrating, they can be dangerous. You might think your spouse is tailgating, driving too fast, or being reckless, but he probably doesn't have a death wish. Your backseat driving may actually distract the driver, placing you all at risk. Your need to help prevent an accident may be the thing that causes one. As a couple, try implementing some of these tools that experts suggest help combat this nagging habit:

1. Make your backseat driver aware of the dangers.
2. Tell them how you feel.
3. Give them a task.

4. Plan your trip.
5. Find something to listen to.
6. Consider changing your driving style.[3]

Making backseat drivers aware of the dangers is sometimes all it takes. Instead of arguing, or yelling at your spouse, use self-control to say something like, "Amber, I'm aware of the cars around me and I'm going the speed limit. It may feel like I'm going too fast to you, but I'm not. When you screech at me, it may cause an accident. Please trust me to get us to our destination safely."

It's easy to assume our spouses know how we feel, but that's not always the case. Outside of conflict, and preferably off the road, let your spouse know that her nagging and fretting is hurtful. Kindly offer her reassurance about your track record and ask her to make an attempt to curb her comments. None of us wants to hurt each other, but sometimes we aren't aware how emotionally draining our backseat driving can become to our spouse on the receiving end. Feelings of helplessness are often at play with backseat drivers. Most of us rely on navigational systems to point us in the right direction, but enlisting your spouse as the official navigator can help her feel more in control and give her something to focus on other than your driving.

I agree with the experts that putting a plan in place goes a long way toward a smooth drive. If both of you know the path you are about to take, it rules out questioning and confusion. Do a quick check-in with each other so you know the best route to take, eliminating some of your arguments. And backseat drivers, it's perfectly okay to take the scenic route. Let your spouse make choices for himself, showing him respect. You can sit back and determine to enjoy the ride, even if it's not the route you would normally take.

Some of our best drives are the ones where we are listening to an audiobook or podcast. Anything that can take your minds off the need to tell each other what to do is a good strategy. Being entertained and interested in what you are listening to also gives you something to bond over instead of wasting time feeling triggered by one another's driving skills.

As I shared before, I have taken some of Amber's concerns to heart. I did tend to take my driving a little too casually and I have worked hard to correct that. Amber has made great strides in her tone of voice and level of trust when she's in the passenger seat. Both of us have come a long way, but only because we didn't dig in our heels, resisting one another's views.

I love Amber and I want her to know that I hear her and her concerns, even when she is pushing my buttons. I must look beyond my own pride and embarrassment and realize that I have a responsibility that she entrusts to me every single time I get behind the wheel. We have four precious little guys sitting in the backseat. They are the inspiration for us to work on these triggers in loving ways. We don't just want to provide a safe environment on the road for our family, but to set the tone through our interactions for the time when our boys someday will learn to drive themselves. With that in mind, we put the brakes on our angry reactions. Our example to them as we travel from place to place helps us keep our cool. Get on board with being a flexible, humble, and loving passenger, and take to heart the advice of your spouse when it's your turn behind the wheel, and you won't just have smooth sailing, you'll put love in the driver's seat.

Let's Pray: "Dear God, I come before You to ask for Your guidance and calming influence in dealing with our frustrations with each other's driving. Help us to communicate lovingly while we are on the road. We both want safety for our family and we both want to glorify You in the way we approach each other in love. Allow me to have more control over my tongue. Help me to not be quick to offense when my husband/wife tries to tell me how to drive. Keep us safe on the road, but protect our hearts from angry outbursts or feelings of fear. Thank You, Jesus! Amen!"

CHAPTER 4

WHEN FINANCES CAUSE YOU TO CLASH (AMBER)

A reader named Meredith recently wrote to me for advice about a sticky financial situation she and her husband suddenly found themselves in. Though her exact situation may be different from the one you are facing in your marriage, the path to navigating this painful trigger biblically is universal. Take a look at what she shared with me:

"Dear Amber, my husband and I have come so far in our relationship, but I am incredibly hurt by something my husband did and although my heart forgives him, my brain is still trying to understand why it happened.

"We have separate accounts for our bank, and he uses his to pay bills. Our $6,000 tax return was mistakenly deposited into his account instead of our joint account. We'd made plans for finally paying off some debt and medical bills for our daughter who has health issues. Instead, he spent it all on himself, purchasing items he wanted but didn't need. It's February (Valentine's Day) and he didn't do anything for me. He said I must not have forgiven him since I am not lovey-dovey with him, but this is a fresh wound. I don't think he should expect me to get over it in a day or two. I'm a gifts and acts-of-service person—that's what makes me feel loved—so I feel the least he could do is say he is sorry by trying to be helpful around the house.

"I want so badly to let it go, but I don't know how. He tells me not everyone is like me, thinking of others first, but does that excuse what he did? Please pray for me, for him, for our family."

Can you hear the pain in her voice? It's obvious that though the financial loss was hard, the *personal wound* she felt from her husband's actions and attitude was the real sorrow. Meredith felt forgotten. Betrayed. Unimportant. She was searching for understanding. For justice. The anger she felt was righteous in that she was grieving over the sin of self-centeredness she saw in her spouse, but the danger is that her indignation could easily turn to bitterness and other angry reactions—also symptoms of unrighteous anger.

Meredith's runaway thoughts may have been justified, but they stirred up a storm cloud of angst. She was in danger of allowing the root of unforgiveness and self-pity to hurt her marriage even further. Most of us sympathize with Meredith's situation, but our responses in times like these must reflect our faith in God and desire to act with grace, even when it's painful. Instead of heaping our own angry reactions onto our spouses, we are able to offer supernatural responses that benefit us far more than vengeful outbursts or cold shoulders. As Christ-followers we are called to exchange blessings for curses, love for hatred, kindness for hostility, generosity for selfishness. It's a holy barter, impossible to live out without allowing the love of God to live within. Justice doesn't always offer healing, but godly grace always does.

It's important to ask ourselves some poignant questions when conflicts over finances (or any other issue) arise:

Justice doesn't always offer healing, but godly grace always does.

What is my goal in dealing with this issue?

Am I opening my heart to understanding my spouse's point of view? Can I let go of my need in this situation for the betterment of my spouse/marriage? Am I being humble? Is what I am saying and thinking biblical? What verses would support my approach? Convict me of my approach?

If we don't come to a place of agreement or understanding, am I willing to yield?

Can I grace my spouse and give him what he doesn't deserve, just as Jesus does for me so often?

Keep in mind that timing is everything. When peace rules our hearts, that is the moment to hash things out and set some specific plans in place. When emotions are high, few of us can become teachable or communicate in a way that has the other person's best interest wholly in mind. Our emotions block us from thinking logically or responding gently and biblically.

In the introduction, we talked about identifying your trigger moments as much as identifying the triggers themselves. Are financial discussions one of your trigger moments? Do you cringe every time the topic of money comes up? A good idea is to decide with your spouse that you will talk about finances only when you have the budget right in front of you or only on the weekend when your schedules are more "relaxed." Coming to these kinds of agreements with one another is a proactive way to avoid the reactive disagreements we all want to avoid.

Eventually, Meredith wrote to let me know that she and her

husband had a chance to talk after she had taken some time to privately process her grievances. While her husband still did not fully grasp the impact of his choices, they were making headway toward healing. Clearly, they have some work to do to open communication, have accountability, and be sacrificial in their day-to-day care for one another. But, giving up the desire to make someone pay for his or her mistakes does not let that person off the hook. It frees you to hate the sin and love the sinner. (We in no way condone outright abuse or controlling and ongoing sinful behaviors surrounding money or any other issue. Grace does not equate to allowing sinful behavior to go unchecked. In these kinds of severe marital problems, we encourage you to get support and help from professionals.)

For any of us dealing with financial issues, forgiveness, and mercy, a commitment to move forward toward better practices may involve counseling or enrolling in a Christian-based financial planning program. The key is to be inclusive of one another's ideas and feelings, working toward a reasonable and godly practice of stewardship. It sounds simple enough, but we forget that money is never more important than the people in our lives. But what if your spouse refuses to collaborate with you? What if he/she is not open to working together or understanding your views on this topic? In our book *Parenting Scripts: When What You're Saying Isn't Working, Say Something New,* my co-author Wendy Speake writes:

"There's only one person God gave you the power to control and that's yourself. You do you."

You do you. God is more interested in our own transformation than He is in fixing our circumstances so that we don't have to change. When your husband disregards your feelings about spending, commit to being mindful of his feelings. When your wife forgets to balance the checkbook, be diligent on your end. You can never go wrong by doing what is right! Our prayer is that every spouse comes to a place of maturity and desires to be part of a team, willing to work toward a better marriage, but you and I can only control our own choices, not theirs. This is the time to put into practice 1 Peter 4:19:

"So then, those who suffer according to God's will should entrust their souls to their faithful Creator and continue to do good."

Are you doing God's will, trying to do the right thing, in spite of your spouse's sin or neglect over finances? Then entrust yourself to God and continue to do the next right thing as much as it depends on you. Do good. Pray for your husband or wife. Then leave the rest to your "faithful Creator." Actively wait in expectation that God will answer. The goal of this chapter is not to hash out all the ways that husbands and wives can avoid financial pitfalls, but instead to offer some insight into how we can respond in a godly way when these battles over bills arise. Because for most of us it's not an "if," it's a "when."

In fact, the issue of money is mentioned more than 800 times throughout the Bible. The words "love" and "sin" are each referred to half as many times as money! Why does God put such an emphasis on this topic? For good reason. Matthew 6:21 (NIV) reminds us: "For where your treasure is, there your heart will be also." Whatever we do with our money is a reflection of our hearts. If we are generous givers, neither putting too much emphasis on our bank accounts or being neglectful of them, it reveals several things:

We trust in God to supply all our needs. (Philippians 4:19)
We have a heart of obedience. (I Timothy 6:17–19)
We are believers. (1 Timothy 5:8)

We care about others. (I John 3:17–18)

We understand the hope of eternity. (Matthew 6:19–21)

We place our security in God, not things. (Luke 12:33–34)

We are content. (Hebrews 13:5)

We desire to live righteously. (1 Timothy 6:10)

We are devoted to God. (Matthew 6:24)

We give honor to God. (Proverbs 3:9–10)

This list could go on and on. There is no shortage of character traits that money reveals about us and our beliefs about God. For Guy and me, money has certainly exposed our hearts. The tension of anxiety has often rocked our marriage. As business owners in the entertainment industry, a steady income is often elusive. We sacrificed just about everything—including our beautiful home and my old, but cherished, sports car—to get our company off the ground. I don't think we are the only ones who experience this kind of tumult, but personally, it's easy for me to stop trusting God and become discontent.

My first job was teaching sixth grade in a sweet little Christian school in Los Angeles. The day my first paycheck came in, I splurged and bought a beautiful gold bracelet with interlocking rings. It symbolized years of hard work and achievement. I wore it every day for many years. Several years into our marriage, we'd experienced a major economic recession and a job loss and had two little ones in diapers, and I knew that I needed to sell my bracelet to make ends meet. The price of gold was unusually high, so I took my beloved trinket and sold it to a local jeweler.

I was glad to provide for my family but heartbroken over selling something so precious to me for a short-term fix. I told myself that I didn't blame anybody for our circumstances, but my loss harbored feelings of resentment toward God and my husband. Life didn't feel "fair" every time I instinctively reached into my jewelry box to slip on my bracelet only to be reminded of our financial crisis. I wallowed in my misery long enough to realize that it wasn't doing me—or my relationship with Guy—any good. I was allowing something temporal and ultimately insignificant to rob me of my joy in the Lord.

How silly I was to allow a bracelet to take my joy! My Jesus, your Jesus, is right beside us, providing, protecting, loving. When righteous anger fills our hearts, He searches our souls to guard us against the co-mingling of unrighteous anger. If our spouse resists change or carries on unwisely in financial decisions, He helps us to respond with loving-kindness and discernment. When worry and discontent threaten to discourage us, Jesus is ready to offer us peace and satisfaction. When everything and everyone seems unstable, Jesus remains steadfast. Put your trust in Him to both refine you and meet your needs, and you will find a security that is far more valuable than money.

Let's Pray: "Heavenly Father, You are our Provider. I trust You to cover our financial needs. Forgive me for my lack of faith. My views about money have often been sinful, and I need Your help to manage and steward the money You have given to me and my spouse. Grant us Your wisdom. Allow financial discussions to bring us together instead of tearing us apart. Help us to be loving and generous when it comes to finances because You love a cheerful giver. All we have is Yours, Lord. May our finances reflect our desire to love and serve You. In Jesus' Name, Amen."

CHAPTER 5

WHEN LIFE GETS TOO BUSY (AMBER)

*I*t's called a rat race for good reason. Trying to balance work and home life can make us feel like we are trapped in a maze, scurrying around from one event or appointment to the next, rarely slowing down to enjoy the world or the people around us. I don't know about you, but when there is no room for margin, the world feels like it's pressing in, suffocating me. That's not exactly the state of mind for giving gentle biblical responses when I'm triggered.

We are living in an epidemic of busyness. Readers tell me all the time that they know they are too busy; they just don't know how to change that. They acknowledge that when the hustle and bustle of life overtakes them, they are quick to express anger and frustration. For those of us with kids, their behavior is a good barometer for when we need to slow down. Children become grumpy and overtired, and their immunity runs down if we are doing too much. We have experienced this in the Lia household too. It's bad enough when Guy and I are fussy, but adding four boys who have been pushed beyond their limits can make our household a hotbed for angry reactions all around. The stress of so many obligations, responsibilities, and pressures of everyday life takes its toll on us physically, emotionally, and spiritually.

As I write this chapter, it's December, and yesterday was the beginning of a new week. I woke up ready to tackle the day, but a few hours in, my vision blurred. I blinked my eyes, praying that what I suspected was about to happen was just my imagination. It wasn't. I hurried to get my son set up on my laptop for an online homeschool class and then rushed to nurse our toddler down for his nap, all the while bracing myself for the agony I knew would hit in the next twenty minutes. Guy was off at a meeting with some writers for a TV show we are staffing, so I was on my own. Sure enough, the migraine hit me like a ton of bricks.

Within minutes, I became incapacitated and felt the delirium press in as I texted Guy to let him know that I was fading. I never even made it to my bed before the nausea hit me. Guy came home to find me on the floor, shivering. After half a day in bed, I surfaced, very slowly, to check on everyone. Migraines are rare for me, but this one was no surprise—my biggest trigger is stress. The deadline for this book is looming, my kids have been sick, we experienced a financial debacle the week before, and Guy and I are involved in high-pressure negotiations for a major deal with a TV network. The boys added both parkour and art classes to our weekly schedule, and I have spent hours trying to sort out new curricula for the spring semester. Both our cars broke down at the exact same time, wreaking havoc on an already full agenda. December is a month for celebrating the birth of Jesus, but for us, it was giving birth to lots of extra pressure. I thought I was handling all the responsibilities well, but my body told the real story—I was too busy and too stressed.

What's worse is that Guy and I had a huge argument during the tumultuous chaos of those manic days. Our busy and stressful lives aren't just revealed by migraines. They show up in the form of snapping at one another and taking each other for granted. If we become so busy that our spouse becomes a bother to us instead of being a treasure, then we have a problem. In the past, this kind of schedule would have caused distance between us for many months. I would have stewed in my anger and frustration, and Guy would have turned mean-spirited, saying things that hurt my feelings. Nowadays, we still face the trigger of when we get too busy, but we know better, so we behave better.

This may sound simple, but one of the first things we must do when we are triggered by being too busy is pursue rest. It's my belief that especially in the Western world, our enemy, Satan, seeks to distract us from specific things God has asked us to do to combat busy schedules and high stress. When we run from one thing to the next, and fill our weekends with so-called leisure activities, it's easy to ignore one of God's key examples of how He desires His children to live. Genesis 2:2–3 (NIV) says:

"By the seventh day God had finished the work he had been doing; so on the seventh day he rested from all his work. Then God blessed the seventh day and made it holy, because on it he rested from all the work of creating that he had done."

If resting is good for God, then it's good for us. Neither Guy nor I rest well. It has become a spiritual discipline, one we are still working at, to be intentional to rest. Because we are self-employed, our schedules are always in flux. We must be all the more disciplined to carve out time to rest. Some of you have long hours at work, keeping you away from the family too much. Others are home all day with kids, never getting a minute for yourselves. It's hard to

If resting is good for God, then it's good for us.

imagine how things could change when it all feels necessary. In our home, under-scheduling instead of over-scheduling has become a necessity for a more peaceful home life.

Do you struggle to set down your phones so you can be fully present with your family? How often do you take naps? Or make plans to spend time, on a regular basis, doing nothing at all? When was the last time you felt like you had a handle on your life instead of feeling like your life had a chokehold on you? Our culture values accomplishment, but often at the cost of burnout.

One of the first things I recommend to couples who feel like they live in a state of short-temperedness is to slow down and build intentional rest into their daily lives. When all our energy is spent fighting one another, we are powerless to fight the better fight. Micah 6:8 (MSG) reminds us how to prioritize:

"But he's already made it plain how to live, what to do,
what God is looking for in men and women.
It's quite simple: Do what is fair and just to your neighbor,
be compassionate and loyal in your love,
And don't take yourself too seriously—
take God seriously."

Sounds simple enough, doesn't it? Take a deep, slow breath and exhale with me right now. Now, think about your day. What on your agenda is fair and just? What activities will foster a compassionate spirit in you and your spouse? Do your current responsibilities reveal your loyalty and love for your spouse? Your kids? This passage is a holy filter for everything we do in our lives. If something isn't working or fitting into the Micah 6:8 filter, then it's probably time to prayerfully reevaluate your busy life.

Let me encourage you to do one thing, immediately, that will begin to get you back on track, fulfilling "what is good" and what the Lord requires of you. It's no natural thing, humanly speaking, to treat our neighbors (and spouses) with both justice and mercy. It's supernatural Holy Spirit power that shifts our focus from the myopic nature of our to-do lists to a grander perspective of living each day from a place of compassion, loyalty, love, and dependence on God, but it's an excellent instruction for calming the storms when we feel triggered.

One of the most practical ways that Guy and I find rest is by committing to take our family to church every weekend. There is nothing, and I mean *nothing*, that refreshes the soul and spirit more than worshiping with other believers and being poured into by a godly pastor. Just as our car needs weekly fill-ups at the gas station to keep running smoothly, our souls need weekly refreshment to operate at optimal capacity. For those of you who are part of a healthy church, keep going! Soak in ways to be refreshed by the services and the encouragement you receive from like-minded brothers and sisters in Christ.

I'd like to speak to any couples who do not attend a solid Bible-teaching church for a moment. Please hear my tone of voice when I say this. I'm not pointing any fingers or judging anyone. I have my own sinfulness to deal with and I would never want anyone to feel a sense of guilt from me—but I do want all of us to feel godly conviction so we can move toward Christlikeness. There are many reasons not to attend church, especially when our lives are already busy. Weekends are filled with sports, work, parties,

When all our energy is spent fighting one another, we are powerless to fight the better fight.

and house chores. But this is what I mean by my belief that Satan tries to distract us from the things God knows we need. God asks us to meet, regularly, with the body of Christ. "We should not stop gathering together with other believers, as some of you are doing. Instead, we must continue to encourage each other even more as we see the day of the Lord com-

When was the last time you felt like you had a handle on your life instead of feeling like your life had a chokehold on you? Our culture values accomplishment, but often at the cost of burnout.

ing" (Hebrews 10:25, GWT). There are only a small handful of practices that the Lord asks us to do. He is not a God of religion, but of relationship. God says we need to come together with other believers, and I think He knows what He is talking about!

Another way we find rest and offset the trigger of busyness in our lives is through our community. This is another reason going to church is so important, even if your spouse chooses not to attend with you. Relationships with other believers is a special form of comfort, especially when we fall on hard times. Building relationships with other Christ-followers allows us to fulfill Galatians 6:2 (ESV): "Bear one another's burdens, and so fulfill the law of Christ." We find rest when we allow friends to help us carry our burdens, and we rob others of rest when we are not present to carry theirs. Attending weekly services reminds us that we are not alone. We don't need to go through life isolated. Both God and our brothers and sisters in Christ are there to share the load. If we are taking Micah 6:8 to heart, then attending church and linking arms with others is an important part of finding rest for our souls, taking to heart God's best plan for our lives.

We find rest when we allow friends to help us carry our burdens, and we rob others of rest when we are not present to carry theirs.

Some of us may be in a season of life that necessitates a busier-than-usual schedule. Demands for our time and attention may be unavoidable. But we know that if we continue being testy and irritated with our spouses, we are headed for a crisis if we aren't there already. If we can't change our schedules, we need to change our perspectives. Jesus is our perfect example of living graciously in the busiest seasons of life. During an intense day of meeting the demands of the crowds, He took time to be a Good Shepherd:

"The apostles gathered around Jesus and reported to him all they had done and taught. Then, because so many people were coming and going that they did not even have a chance to eat, he said to them, 'Come with me by yourselves to a quiet place and get some rest.' So they went away by themselves in a boat to a solitary place." (Mark 6:30–32, NIV)

Jesus understands what it's like to be so busy that we don't even have a chance to eat. He led his disciples to a place of rest. But then the people followed him. Jesus viewed them with compassion and began to teach them. As the day waned, one of his disciples suggested they send the people away to find food. Jesus told the disciple to feed the people! After looking around, the disciple came up with five loaves of bread and two fish.

"Then Jesus directed them to have all the people sit down in groups on the green grass . . . Taking the five loaves and the two fish and looking up to heaven, he gave thanks and broke the loaves. Then he gave them to his disciples to distribute to the people. He also divided the two fish among them all. They all ate and were satisfied, and the disciples picked up twelve basketfuls of broken pieces of bread and fish. The number of the men who had eaten was five thousand." (Mark 6:39–44, NIV)

Jesus and His disciples just wanted a little break. It didn't seem too much to ask. And yet, there was no rest for the weary, after all. What was their gentle biblical response? They carried on. They did what needed doing with a right spirit. Jesus had compassion—just as our passage in Micah encourages us to use it as a filter to evaluate our own actions. And in the end, Jesus performed a miracle for the books!

When we are tired and empty, and our resources are dwindling, that's the feeding ground for miracle making. We, too, may have long days, with no end in sight, hungry for rest and hungry for food. Let's not forget that Jesus always satisfies. We don't have to lose our cool, speak harshly with our husbands or wives, or get irritated by all the needs of our people. Anger is a waste of our energy when life gets hectic. The Lord is an unending source of peace and grace for every weary moment.

Let's Pray: "Lord, I'm weary and irritable and triggered. Our lives are too busy! Thank You, Jesus, for Your example of taking time to rest but also being willing to do the right thing even when rest escaped You. I want to release my stress and anxiety to You. Lord, grant me peace. Help my husband/wife and I to be intentional to rest and intentional to slow down. Show us what we need to cut out of our schedules. Forgive me for being short-tempered and help me to cherish my spouse. Lord, I submit to Your plans for my life and release unnecessary burdens that I am holding onto. I offer my time and agenda to You. In Jesus' Name, Amen!"

CHAPTER 6

WHEN YOU NEED TO
PRAY TOGETHER (AMBER)

*I*t's hard to be angry with someone you are fervently praying for. The act of prayer is an expression of love. When we
pray, our love for our spouse has a fighting chance to override
our anger. Unfortunately, when we are frustrated or upset with
our wives or husbands, our first inclination is not usually to stop
and pray for them, much less *with* them.

In my early twenties, I was a gym rat. With no husband or
kids to happily distract me, I finished my workday and made a
beeline for the gym, where I would spend the
It's hard to be next two to three hours weight training with
angry with the likes of former Mr. Olympia winners and
someone you career bodybuilders. I admit that it was a bit
are fervently obsessive, but the appeal of seeing the physi-
praying for. cal transformation from daily exertion under
the extreme pressure of hoisting barbells and
strict discipline drew me in. The camaraderie of the workout
room also provided friendships in which we all had a common
goal: to become stronger.

Though my hard-core gym days are a thing of the past, some of the lessons I learned there are foundational in my life today. If we want transformation in our physical bodies, we must discipline ourselves to effect change. Experts describe muscle growth by explaining that "after your workout, your body repairs or replaces damaged muscle fibers through a cellular process where it fuses muscle fibers together to form new muscle protein strands or myofibrils. These repaired myofibrils increase in thickness and number to create muscle hypertrophy (growth)."[4] Similarly, Bible scholars agree that our prayer life is a spiritual discipline. Dr. Don Whitney, author of *Spiritual Disciplines for the Christian Life*, describes it like this: "The spiritual disciplines are those practices found in Scripture that promote spiritual growth among believers in the gospel of Jesus Christ. They are habits of devotion, habits of experiential Christianity that have been practiced by God's people since biblical times."[5] Exercising prayer builds our spiritual muscles.

But what does this have to do with our marriages? There is no mention of our feelings in the equation of spiritual disciplines. Making time for prayer is a choice. I admit, when my husband triggers me toward anger, it's unnatural for me to stop and consider praying before responding, but as a Christ-follower, I get to operate in supernatural ways. I can create a new habit of prayer in my life, even in the midst of anger and frustration. One of my mottos when I was bodybuilding and feeling lazy and uninspired was this: *I don't have to be motivated. I just have to be disciplined.* When triggers in our marriage seem routine, the power of prayer is a holy disruption to the status quo. That's just what some of us need. Instead of allowing today to look just like tomorrow, we need a prayer disruptor in our relationships. If we can commit to strength training, we can commit to something far more important: the strengthening of our marriages through prayer. Our desire to pray for our spouse will increase as we make it a habit and a go-to discipline, instead of reverting to the same old angry reactions.

In the middle of a conflict, Guy and I are often relieved when one of us tells the other that we see the conversation escalating and we need to stop. We have agreed that when things start to go in an unhealthy direction, we can both table the issue until we can be calm. We take time apart to breathe, think clearly, and pray. When we come back together, we are in a much better place to listen, show kindness, and problem-solve instead of arguing. It's a good idea to reunite and say a prayer together before rehashing the issue, simply saying:

"Lord, we don't want to hurt one another. Help us put one another's needs before our own. Open our hearts to understanding and allow us to be loving as we work this out. Give us wisdom. In Jesus' Name, Amen!"

If your marriage triggers seem overwhelming, put this one habit into place, and you will see the power of prayer in ways you never imagined! You see, the people we pray for are the people we care about. We are willing to go before the Lord on their behalf because they matter to us. Conversations with God are our most intimate moments, so to speak to Him for the benefit of someone else is one of the most loving things we can do. A marriage where two people continually practice loving actions is one that cannot help but move in the right direction.

> *When triggers in our marriage seem routine, the power of prayer is a holy disruption to the status quo.*

When feelings of love or affection are being overshadowed by our problems, prayer is foundational in reversing our angry reactions and setting us up for gentle responses. In the heat of our anger, our flesh is at work. Prayer ushers us into operating by the Spirit: "The mind governed by the flesh is death, but the mind governed by the Spirit is life and peace" (Romans 8:6, NIV). I don't know about you, but when my husband and I are arguing or our feelings are hurt, it feels like a little death inside my heart. In the past, I have mistakenly believed that I would feel better if I won the argument. Jesus is our Redeemer and He came to give us life to the full. When I take my hurt to Him in prayer, He heals my wounded heart, restores and refreshes my spirit, calms my scattered thinking, and allows me to focus on my own spiritual growth instead of the wrongdoing of my husband. Victory is not taking the upper hand in a heated discussion; it's allowing the Lord to infuse us with His wisdom and character in the middle of conflict.

A marriage where two people continually practice loving actions is one that cannot help but move in the right direction.

For some of us, prayer is not something we feel confident doing. The disciples asked Jesus to teach them how to pray. We can do the same. I love the subheading the publisher of the Easy-to-Read Version of the Bible includes for Luke 11. It says, "Ask God for What You Need." We want to spend time thanking God for the blessings in our lives, but He also encourages us to ask Him for what we need. Maybe we need God to give us a more positive outlook on our marriage. Or we may need God to soften our spouse's heart to an idea we have been suggesting. Maybe we need God to help us hold our tongue. Luke 11:11–13 (ERV) says:

"What would you do if your son asked you for a fish? Would any father give him a snake? Or, if he asked for an egg, would you give him a scorpion? Of course not! Even you who are bad know how to give good things to your children. So surely your heavenly Father knows how to give the Holy Spirit to the people who ask him."

Praying for our marriage relationship to be all that God designed it to be is a prayer that God longs to answer. He is a good Father! He gives good gifts to us, His children. The Holy Spirit is our Counselor and our Helper. We need not live in turmoil, triggered, or hopeless when we have direct and immediate access to God in prayer. As long as we can pray, we can have hope:

When the righteous cry for help, the Lord hears and delivers them out of all their troubles. (Psalm 34:17, ESV)

Take a moment and reflect on your most common trigger in your own marriage. How do you typically react? How does your spouse react? Are your reactions helping or hurting? Imagine your home becoming one where one spouse continually encourages the other to step away from heated arguments to stop and become calm and pray. Now, imagine your home as a place where both of you put down your boxing gloves and yield to praying for one another instead of continuing with a war of words or shutting down and becoming isolated. With God, nothing is impossible. Perhaps your first prayer is simply, "Lord, help us to become a couple who prays together."

I have a handful of old pictures from my weight-training days. I look at that young lady and see the definition of muscles I worked so hard to build. They serve as a reminder to me that you cannot be engaged in the act of exercising muscles and not see results. The same is true if we want to build strong marriages.

Praying for our husbands or wives is a demonstration of both discipline and love. When we are disciplined to love our spouse through prayer, we plug into the supernatural and all-powerful strength of God Almighty. How could we not be changed as a result? God is not a promise breaker! We have nothing to lose when we commit to praying with our spouses. We have only healthy, godly marriages to gain.

Let's Pray: "Heavenly Father, You are a good Father. You long to help us deal with our triggers biblically and lovingly. We struggle with anger and frustration. Help us to stop when we begin to argue or become closed off to one another. Lord, give us a desire to pray for one another. Stop us from wounding each other and instead heal us and help us to become a couple whose first thought is to pray for one another. Thank You, Lord, for being our strength when we feel weak. Overcome our triggers with Your grace and Truth. Help us make this a new and life-changing habit. In Jesus' Name, Amen!"

CHAPTER 7

WHEN IN-LAWS CAUSE FRICTION (GUY)

Kyle and Kate decided to attend college in different states, promising one another to make the most of school breaks and regular phone calls. They continued dating long distance with the hope that after graduation, they would start their lives together. Once they both completed college and moved back home, things felt a little strained, but that was to be expected; they had ground to make up. Kyle already had Kate's father's blessing to ask Kate to be his wife and he planned to propose later that summer. Both families couldn't wait for the high school sweethearts to make it official.

As the summer months ended, Kyle planned a special dinner date for Kate. He had the engagement ring with him just in case the time felt right. When he got to the restaurant, Kyle could feel Kate's uneasiness. Something was up. She proceeded to tell him that a few months before graduation, she met a guy and had been dating him off and on for the last six months. She wanted to end her relationship with Kyle. He sat stunned as she placed her napkin on the table and left.

Over the next few years, Kyle dedicated himself to his work.

He took to the outdoors, finding solace in God and the world around him. Kate became a memory. Kyle's parents and siblings urged him to try and reconnect with Kate after her new relationship came to an end. It seemed that they were having a much harder time moving on than he did.

Eventually, Kyle started dating Anne, a young woman from church who was athletic, outdoorsy, and artistic—very different from Kate. Anne had a fantastic career as a physician's assistant and was a deeply caring person. Even though he'd never thought he would be able to fall in love again, he did. His family was polite, but they didn't warm up to her the way they had with Kate. When Kyle proposed, they were less than enthusiastic. After the wedding, they became downright cold.

Kyle never understood why his mom and dad, normally loving people, didn't connect with Anne. They weren't unkind; they simply didn't embrace her in the way Kyle hoped they would. Still friends with Kate's parents, Kyle's parents kept Anne at arm's length. They never engaged in deep conversation about her with Kyle and avoided conversations about his marriage. Even Kyle's brothers and sisters avoided being a part of Anne's world. Kyle's love for Anne was stronger than ever. He knew God had not made a mistake and that his family was missing out on being a part of their marriage. Resigned, he settled for making the most of his immediate family with Anne and cherishing her as his wife.

Despite the pain his extended family was causing, Kyle was living out Matthew 19:5 (BSB): "'For this reason a man will leave his father and his mother and be united to his wife, and they will become one flesh.' So they are no longer two, but one flesh. Therefore, what God has joined together, let no one separate."

The significance of Matthew 19:5 outlines God's specific and intimate plan for marriage—a relationship that should be stronger than any other earthly relationship. One that is our responsibility to protect! Not always easy, is it?

While it hurt that Kyle's family kept a distance, he knew that his focus needed to be on Anne. They missed sharing in the family holidays and special occasions. Anne, who should have felt very unloved and rejected, let the Holy Spirit be her comfort. Kyle's love and commitment to her made all the difference. When kids came along, they focused on creating the kind of family environment they longed for. Anne hoped that someday, the family dynamic would improve. Meanwhile she had her own family and traditions, and that was enough. Though Kyle and Anne handled their circumstances well, the tensions in their family caused triggers—an unfortunate set of obstacles that they had to work through and overcome together.

Kyle and Anne's story is not unusual. In other cases, in-laws demand too much involvement and want to interject with every little decision couples make for their families. Mothers-in-law can become too involved or critical and fathers-in-law can be demanding. Sometimes, in-laws disrespect their sons and daughters' wishes for how to treat the grandkids, spoiling them or treating them too harshly. Each circumstance offers incredibly challenging situations that can drive a deep wedge between a couple, especially newlyweds who have not yet had an opportunity to establish their own family unit.

Historically, new couples would often leave their families for a year or more in order to avoid any interference at all:

"If a man has recently married, he must not be sent to war or have any other duty laid on him. For one year he is to be free to stay at home and bring happiness to the wife he has married." (Deuteronomy 24:5, NIV)

Those are words that every couple should take to heart! Note who we should be pleasing (wife) and who is not mentioned (in-laws). Extended family can be a blessing, but let's not lose focus on who God sets up as our priority.

One of the most difficult elements of this relational exchange is that spouses feel torn between their loyalties. This often triggers deep anger, resentment, and broken or damaged marriages. What a relief to know that all that angst doesn't have to trigger us! God has already given us a divine road map for navigating these often rocky relationships. Amber says that we can either add to the burden of pressure our spouse feels by our in-laws or we can lighten the load by cultivating peace with our in-laws. Within in-law relationships, we can be used as a trigger or a testimony. Which do you think is the gentle biblical response?

Amber and I experienced some of this early on with our own families, and while we love them dearly, the incredible stresses we were under as a newlywed couple with moves, job changes, and pregnancy within the first few months of our marriage amounted to a difficult start. Our in-law relationships could have been a rich blessing; instead they were one more obstacle for us to navigate. As we look into the future, we would do well to consider how we can be in-laws that both respect and encourage our own future daughters- and sons-in-law to create their own unique bond.

> *Within in-law relationships, we can be used as a trigger or a testimony.*

Kyle and Anne chose to be willing to pray for their family and be an example of grace and love to them for as long as it took. Eventually, their steadfast love and commitment to pray for their families paid off, and they now enjoy the relationships they had lost for many years.

Looking at the life of Jesus, He often extended this same type of love and respect to those who disagreed with Him and even those who hated Him. When questioned by the Pharisees time and time again and knowing their motivation was to catch Him in a statement that would give them the right to jail or even kill Him, Jesus always responded with gentleness and respect; He never allowed His anger to be sinful.

In-law stereotypes are stereotypes for a reason. Their often-negative influence is so pervasive that they are portrayed as caricatures in TV and film. But the pain many of us experience from these challenging relationships isn't a scene from a script, it's a real-life trigger. If this has been an issue for you, choose to spend your energy on protecting your marriage and be an example of Jesus' loving-kindness toward your in-laws. This may be very hard for some of us to do, but it is the godly response.

James 3:17–18 (ESV) is a guiding light for those of us triggered by our in-law relationships:

"But the wisdom from above is first pure, then peaceable, gentle, open to reason, full of mercy and good fruits, impartial and sincere. And a harvest of righteousness is sown in peace by those who make peace."

Are you willing to make peace and reap the reward of a "harvest of righteousness"? It may mean supporting your wife by asking your mother to call before she drops by your home. It might require you to kindly say to your sister-in-law, "We appreciate that you want our kids to be obedient, and we do too, but we prefer more gentle parenting methods."

Pray for wisdom about healthy boundaries, but if in-laws

have been creating friction for some time, you may have a root of bitterness, or a poor attitude about involving them in your lives. Ephesians 4:29, 31–32 (NIV) offers how we should begin to gently and biblically think about our extended family:

"Do not let any unwholesome talk come out of your mouths, but only what is helpful for building others up according to their needs, that it may benefit those who listen. Get rid of all bitterness, rage and anger, brawling and slander, along with every form of malice. Be kind and compassionate to one another, forgiving each other, just as in Christ God forgave you."

As Christ-followers, we can't please all the people all the time. But when we focus on pleasing the Lord, blessings follow. Even in the midst of the most challenging of relationships, we are not helpless or left to figure things out on our own. Allow the Holy Spirit to influence your responses and attitudes. God is the ultimate relationship expert. Apply His commands for loving others and the anger you feel will give way to blessings.

Let's Pray: "Dear Lord God, we want good relationships with our in-laws. We recognize that we can only control our own thoughts and actions. Purify our hearts, Lord! We want to honor You and glorify You, but we are sinners, bent on prideful anger and set off by treatment we do not feel we deserve. Please, Lord, help us to be wise in our communications and loving in our approach, but also resolute in the protection of our family. Thank You, Lord, for Your loving example of how You treat those who mistreat You. Our desire is to be more like You, and we cherish Your presence and favor in these things, Lord. Restore healthy and godly relationships with our in-laws. In Jesus' name we pray, Amen!"

CHAPTER 8

WHEN YOUR LIFE LOOKS DIFFERENT THAN YOU THOUGHT IT WOULD (AMBER)

My friend Amy lived the fairy-tale married life until she found out she was pregnant with quadruplets. Hospitalized early on in her pregnancy, she and her husband, Phil, scrambled, preparing for their lives to turn upside down. As if having three little boys and a daughter in one fell swoop wasn't challenging enough, at age two, their precious son Jordan faced the fight of his life when he was diagnosed with leukemia. Their fairy tale barely had a chance.

For years, Amy and Phil lived on the fragile edge of the unknown. They rejoiced when Jordan entered remission, only to face the fears and trials of a new epilepsy diagnosis, and then at age eleven, the dreaded relapse of leukemia. Their family was often separated as mom and dad played tag team between lengthy hospital stays and caring for Jordan's siblings at home. Trying to manage the practical and emotional needs of one another took a toll. The stress and strain of family life triggered arguments and left almost no time to nurture their own relationship. They wondered if they would ever feel like a normal, happy husband and wife again. Life had turned out much, much different than they'd expected.

For many of us who can relate to Amy and Phil, we might not even recognize our anger as it is often layered under discontent, fear, or anxiety. When our reality is at odds with our hopes and dreams, we become hard to please. Nothing our spouse does is acceptable because we are living in a perpetual place of discomfort. If we really want to have better marriages, then we must be open to self-examination. Let's ask ourselves a few questions. Are we complaining to others about our spouses? Are we negative minded? Do we have a critical spirit? Sometimes, these are the telltale signs of an angry heart. Discovering this about ourselves is no reason to feel guilt or shame if we allow the discovery to push us toward spiritual growth.

Wishing things were different consumes valuable energy that we could be using to pour our hearts out to God in prayer, logically think through possible solutions, or spend ourselves in the sacrificial love of caring for our spouses. Proverbs 3:6 (NASB) says: "In all your ways acknowledge Him, And He will make your paths straight." Our paths may not be what we expect, but that doesn't mean that God has made a mistake.

The Bible is chock-full of stories about people whose lives did not turn out like they thought they would. Mary and Joseph, the earthly parents of Jesus, stand out as examples. Never in a million years would they have predicted that God would choose them to raise the man who would one day become their Savior. Job was sitting pretty until everything and everyone he held most dearly to him was taken in the blink of an eye. David's career trajectory had him on the path to become head shepherd at best and yet he became one of the most valiant kings, devoted to God and used greatly to lead and protect the Israelite nation. Jonah must have pondered the purpose of his life in the belly of the whale, and no doubt Paul was continually amazed that he who had once persecuted Christians was radically saved on the road to Emmaus, living out the rest of his days proclaiming the gospel he once labored to destroy. Can you identify with this long list of God's people?

My own life has not turned out as I expected. Writing this book is another perfect example. A literature teacher, I dreamed of writing the next great American novel. Instead, God has me writing nonfiction, confessing my own history of anger and frustration in marriage and parenting. Nor would I have ever imagined working alongside my husband as we run our production company, producing family- and faith-friendly TV shows and films. I wasn't prepared for kids with learning challenges or the loss of our fourth and fifth children through miscarriage. As my walk with the Lord has grown over the years, so has my ability to trust God's path for me and for my marriage. My peace is not so easily up for grabs and my experiences have shown me that what may look like an impossible situation is not impossible with God. That truth calms my heart, makes me slow to anger and slow to speak words that will hurt my husband or sabotage our relationship. I wish I had learned those lessons sooner.

If our lives don't turn out as we expected, whether good or bad, it can unsettle us. Some of us handle that better than others, but when our expectations come up empty, it causes us to question who we are and what our purpose is. In times like these, I have had to ask myself if I believe that what God says is true. Recently, I had a heartfelt conversation with my friend Amy, and she boiled it down to this: "When I thought I was going to lose my son and my life did not look anything like I desired, I had to ask myself if I really believed God was still good. And that was the conclusion I came to. He *is* good! I believe God is where my joy comes from. It's not in the absence of suffering. It's found in the presence of God, even when my son is so sick. Even when my marriage is weak. God is still good. I have to stand firm and wait for God to do what only God can do. We know that God's grace sustained us before and it will sustain us now."

Amy's words sound a lot like hope to me. The heart growing in hope is not easily triggered. Whenever godly qualities, like hope, increase in our lives, ungodly qualities, like unrighteous anger, diminish. Pastor and author Bill Johnson says that "it may be possible to measure a person's hope by measuring their joy." He explains that biblical hope is defined as "the joyful anticipation of good." Johnson shares that this kind of joy is possible before the outcome of your circumstances concludes. He asks a telling question: "How many of you are tired of being impacted by the size of a problem and you want to impact your problem with the size of your hope?"[6]

As believers, the way we deal with our problems should be so radically different from those who have no hope that they wonder what's wrong with us. It's not about burying our heads in the sand or pretending that life doesn't sometimes throw us for a loop. Hope that comes from God is genuine, deeply rooted in our knowledge that God is good, and He is *for* us. If you don't believe that the present circumstances in your marriage are for your good, then you are under the influence of a lie. That's something worth getting angry over! Directing our anger toward whom it is due, Satan in all his deception, is the only appropriate trigger when life turns out differently than we thought it would.

If you don't believe that the present circumstances in your marriage are for your good, then you are under the influence of a lie.

Mary, Joseph, Job, David, Jonah, and Paul would never have been used by the Lord in such magnificent ways if they had not ultimately put their hope in God. As Amy suggested, each one had to "stand firm and wait for God to do what only God could do." The same is true for you and me.

What a waste it would be to live in a state of anger or bitterness while we wait, when God tells us that we can receive hope and joy, right now, in this very moment, regardless of our circumstances! How many of us reading this chapter have put our spouses through much difficulty because we placed our hope on the events of this earth or in sinful people instead of in Jesus? How many of us are hard to please, unwilling to be a source of joy to our spouses? Which of us is allowing our path to dictate our feelings instead of inviting God to stabilize them? The heart growing in hope is not easily triggered. This is my prayer for you: "May the God of hope fill you with all joy and peace in believing, so that by the power of the Holy Spirit you may abound in hope" (Romans 15:13, ESV).

Take a moment and reflect on your image of life after marriage *before* saying "I do." How is it different now from what you pictured? If it's not the ideal scenario you hoped for, is there some anger residing in your heart? How is that evidenced in your physical well-being? Your emotional stability? Are you heartsick? Easily irritated? Stressed from straining against what you can't change? Resigned? *Hopeless?*

We may not have control over how our lives have turned out, but we always have the power to make the best of the life we have. We always have a choice to trust God with the circumstances of our lives. What if Mary's response to the angel bearing news of her imminent birth had not been, "Truly I am the Lord's servant. Let everything you have said happen to me." (Luke 1:38, ISV) What if Job had not yielded to God and missed out on the double blessing and restoration of all he had lost? What if David had felt inadequate to face Goliath or Jonah had not obeyed God by warning Nineveh of their pending doom? What if Paul had not seen the light? None of them would have received the incredible blessings of God's better plans for them. They would have missed out on opportunities that were far better than any they could have imagined, even

> *We may not have control over how our lives have turned out, but we always have the power to make the best of the life we have.*

though it was often painful to get there. One day, we will understand why things turned out the way they did. Today is not that day. Today is the day for trusting God.

We can either survey the twists and turns of our lives and become angry, making ourselves and everyone around us more miserable, or we can accept the peace of God and look to Him to make something beautiful out of our lives. Your spouse will fail you. Jobs will come and go. When you can't believe what has happened to your life, take the next step that God lays before you. Make meals, do your work to the best of your ability, speak kindly to your husband or wife, be patient as you wait in line to be seated at a restaurant, send a card to a serviceman or woman oversees, mentor a group of young men, shovel your neighbor's driveway. Do the next right thing in front of you, yielding to God's will for your life. And every time you do, hope rises.

Our fourth son, Quade, was a happy surprise. After suffering the miscarriage of our twins, Guy and I never imagined we would experience a healthy pregnancy again. We certainly were not planning on having another child, but God knew what He was doing. We didn't just add a child to our family, we added incredible joy and delight. This baby has all three of his older brothers and his mom and dad in the palm of his tiny toddler hand. Quade's middle name is Spurgeon, after the great pastor and author Charles H. Spurgeon, whom I have read every day for the last twenty years. One of my favorite excerpts is from an out-of-print devotional, *Day by Day with C. H. Spurgeon*. He writes:

> *"Why go I mourning?"* Psalm 42:9 (KJV)
>
> *"Can you answer this,* believer? Can you find any reason why you are so often mourning instead of rejoicing? Why yield to gloomy anticipations? Who told you that the night would never end in day? Who told you that the winter of your discontent would proceed from frost to frost, from snow and ice, and hail, to deeper snow, and yet more heavy tempest of despair? Don't you know that day follows night, that flood comes after ebb, that spring and summer succeed to winter? Have hope then! Hope now and ever! For God fails not."[7]

These days, Amy and Phil are doing things they haven't done in years. So is Jordan. With the help of new treatments, he hasn't had a seizure in many months . . . Phil and Amy finally get to drop him off at youth group and birthday parties. Their marriage is stronger for having gone through the storm because it forced them to look to the One who would see them through it. "We feel like we are entering The Promised Land," Amy shared with me. It got me thinking. As Christ-followers, any land, any position, any circumstance we are in is "Promised Land" because we get to benefit from all God's promises. Feeling angry and frustrated when we don't get to live the life we want may rob us from experiencing the blessings of God's good plans for our lives.

If you are holding this book in your hands, potential looms before you. We may need to let go of our own versions of our fairy tales, but the exchange may turn out to be the greatest gift of our lives if it allows us to be transformed and renewed in Christ. Like so many faithful people before us whose lives were not what they imagined they would be, we have a God who is able to do exceedingly abundantly beyond all we could ask or imagine. On the mountaintop or in the valley, hope in God is ours for the taking. Hope on. Hope ever. Your story isn't over yet.

Let's Pray: "God, my life is not at all what I thought it would be and neither is my marriage. None of this is a surprise to You. Thank You for never leaving me or abandoning me. I trust that Your plans for my life are good—better than mine. Father, give me hope. I yield the picture of what I thought my life would look like to You. I don't want to be bitter about my life. I want to be better. Remove my anger. My frustrations. Stop my wandering thoughts and all my 'what if's.' Help me to see Your goodness and wait on You. Let me be a good and godly wife/husband, even when I'm struggling. Anything is possible with You, Lord! In Jesus' Name, Amen!"

CHAPTER 9

WHEN YOU PARENT DIFFERENTLY (GUY)

*P*arenting expert Dr. James Dobson has been widely quoted as saying, "Children are not casual guests in our home. They have been loaned to us temporarily for the purpose of loving them and instilling a foundation of values on which their future lives will be built."[8] Parenting is then an extension of marriage where a couple calls on God to help them effectively mold, influence, teach, and train their kids. Unfortunately, many couples come into marriage with differing parenting styles that are at odds with one another. The impact can cause a divide in a marriage, a deep disconnection with the children, and an environment where a healthy marriage becomes a strangled mess.

PRAYER

Are you and your spouse parenting on the same page? If not, it's never too late to begin. Because marriage is a union, and unity in parenting is critical. Amber and I have often encouraged you to pray as you deal with your triggers, and we must encourage you to begin with prayer here too. Take a look at 2 Chronicles 7:14 (NIV):

"If my people, who are called by my name, will humble themselves and pray and seek my face and turn from their wicked ways, then I will hear from heaven, and I will forgive their sin and will heal their land."

Anger wounds us and whomever our anger is directed toward. Is there some healing to be had in your marriage? If God says that He will heal the "land" of His people when they turn to Him, humbly seeking His face and turning from their "wicked ways," then we can assume that He will do the same in our homes. There are things in this life that we as humans cannot overcome on our own, and even though we may try, without the Holy Spirit on our side, circumstances can feel insurmountable. Speaking for husbands, as men, we often try to shoulder things ourselves and rely on our own strength. We even misuse our strength in our parenting styles. But when we begin to adopt the gentleness of God in our parenting, we become more like our Heavenly Father, and our children are blessed because of it. Parenting as a unified front begins with praying together for the wisdom and humility to consider one another's perspectives on parenting.

If this is one of your triggers, set a time to talk about your goals as a parent with your spouse. Do your goals reflect the love of Christ? Are they biblical or just based on your

> *If God says that He will heal the "land" of His people when they turn to Him, humbly seeking His face and turning from their "wicked ways," then we can assume that He will do the same in our homes.*

traditions? Take the time to put yourself in your child's shoes. How would you feel if you were being parented in this way? What do you need to reconsider? Come away from your conversation committed to pray for a few days, and then reconvene to discuss what God has placed in your heart.

PLAN

When parents argue in front of or because of their kids, the only thing that is accomplished is division and disunity. Mark 3:25 (NIV) says, "If a house is divided against itself, that house cannot stand." Is that how your house feels? Change occurs only when we put a plan in place. Parenting is no joke; parenting without a plan is ridiculous! Giving birth does not make us great parents. It simply makes us biologically connected. Good parenting comes when we carefully consider how to be good stewards of the gifts God has given to us, and great parenting comes when we parent on the same page!

I remember an episode of the TV show *Supernanny* where a distraught couple was having a difficult time getting their three kids calmed down at bedtime. The boys would fight them when getting their jammies on. They would throw toothpaste at each other and play swords with the toothbrushes. They would eventually get in bed but continue jumping in and out as they laughed and played. After more than an hour of trying to get the boys calmed down and in bed, Mom and Dad would sit down to a cold dinner while the

Good parenting comes when we carefully consider how to be good stewards of the gifts God has given to us, and great parenting comes when we parent on the same page!

kids proceeded to sneak around the house, laughing at their disobedience. Mom and Dad would trade off attempts to get them back to bed, but they had little control and lots of frustration. It was a nightmare!

The main problem was that after the kids ate dinner, Daddy walked in the door from work and got the kids all wound up. It looked like an episode of the *Looney Tunes* cartoon character Tasmanian Devil! Dad, of course, wanted to connect with the kids, and rightfully so, but the way and time in which he did that was counter to Mom's efforts to get the kids wound *down* and ready for bedtime. Instead of creating a calm atmosphere to back up Mom, he reinvigorated the kids. There was no plan, no communication between Mom and Dad, no joint effort to set the kids up for success. By the time the kids were asleep, the opportunity for this couple to have quality time together had dissipated. They fell into a maintenance relationship instead of a loving one. The first step to "fixing" the kids was "fixing" the parents. They needed to come together, express their desires for how their evening should look, and come up with healthier ways to connect and enjoy their children before bedtime.

In *Triggers: Exchanging Parents' Angry Reactions for Gentle Biblical Responses*, Amber discusses the importance of viewing our role of parents as coaches. She writes:

"Let's tweak our parenting perspectives a bit. Perhaps we need to view ourselves more like coaches. A coach is an authority figure, too. A coach is part of a team. A coach doesn't expect the behavior of an Olympic athlete on the first day of practice! An excellent coach sees a weakness and then assigns exercises to train her athletes intentionally."[9]

Parenting requires much practice time on the field, but it also requires much time in the locker room with a blackboard, strategically laying out your steps to begin with. There is a lack of "parenting planning" out there, and not just by individuals but on a larger, more cultural stage. In premarital counseling, most of us have a concentrated focus on finances, in-laws, and sex, but few of us remember talking about differing parenting styles. This means one of the most important roles we can ever play in life, one that has generational implications, is being left to chance and in-the-moment reactions instead of being covered with intentional planning and preparation! More attention is placed on how to have the most comfortable labor and delivery than the actual job of designing a plan for parenting. We spend more time meal planning than planning our parenting approach!

You don't just show up at the hospital and declare that you want to perform surgery. Years of training, trial and error, rigorous exams, sutures on oranges, and then testing in real life are involved before picking up a scalpel.

Psalm 127:3–5 (NIV) says, "Children are a heritage from the Lord, offspring a reward from him. Like arrows in the hands of a warrior are the children born in one's youth. Blessed is the man whose quiver is full of them . . ."

Families are fodder for blessings. A wonderful heritage meant to bring you and your spouse together, not tear you apart. Parenting in the aftermath of issues only breeds anger and frustration, but when you come together with a plan, operating offensively instead of defensively, you are much more apt to enjoy the blessings of your children and your partnership with your spouse.

A good place to begin is to show care and interest in whoever has spent the most time parenting that day. My wife and I have found it beneficial to continue to communicate and reconnect over the day's events related to our children. We all know that the second we get kids down for bed and close the door behind us, the only thing we want to

> *We spend more time meal planning than planning our parenting approach!*

do is the Nestea Plunge onto the couch! However, this is a wonderful time to set aside ten minutes to review the events of the day related to your children, who are in a constant state of transition and growth. Use that time to evaluate what is working and what is not. You don't have to figure everything out. Sometimes it's simply a time to say, "Lord, we aren't sure what to do in this situation, but we know that You promise to give us wisdom. Help us to think creatively and with discernment and let us be unified parents as we raise our kids for You."

PRACTICE

Amber and I want to caution you against becoming too discouraged too quickly as you begin to implement gentle biblical responses toward your children and put on a united front. Amber says, "It takes a childhood to raise a child and a parenthood to learn how best to parent." Practice makes perfect, as the saying goes. However, perfection is not something I imagine ever achieving. One of the lessons I have learned both in sports and in parenting is that no matter how much I do, no matter how many sprints I run or passes I take, no matter how many books I read or how many friends give me advice, the entire game changes once I step onto the field to play. Professional athletes don't stop practicing once the season ends. They still do sprints, run though passing drills, and work on their agility, so why would we ever think trying one thing that may not work is a reason to throw in the towel? Our kids are changing constantly as they mature and develop. Our parenting strategies may as well, but the one constant is to treat our kids as we would want to be treated.

PRESENCE

Your collective presence as husband and wife is a key factor to great parenting; as the saying goes, "You got to be in it, to win it!" Too often I hear or read that women feel alone in parenting. Guys, I am mostly speaking to you here. Even though cultural trends are changing more and more with more women either in the workplace or working from home, most women feel they continue to shoulder the lion's share of responsibility when it comes to parenting. Often women share that they will spend the day molding, educating, loving on, and trouble-shooting with their kids only to have Dad come home and blow it without knowing what transpired throughout the day or even worse, showing a complete and total lack of presence! Sometimes, they see the whirlwind around them and resort to criticism instead of seeking ways to understand. My wife and I call on our way home from work or being out all day to check in and see how things went with the kids. It's always good to know what you are walking into. You can "go home" mentally before you actually arrive home, preparing your heart to be a blessing to your spouse and kids.

Use the commute to consider ways to be a help ahead of time.

By preparing for this journey of parenting and openly communicating about your parenting styles with your spouse, you are staking your claim over your home and your children. Nobody wants to look back on their family and say they parented by accident or on a whim. With prayer as your foundation, love as your inspiration, communication as your tool, and intention as your purpose, those triggers that arise in differing parenting styles can be worked through to get you both moving in the same direction. When you put your heads together for the benefit of your family, you stop wasting your energy on your triggers and start using it on becoming the family God intended, experiencing the richness of the blessings He longs to give you.

Let's Pray: "Dear Lord, we come before You thankful that You have chosen us specifically to parent these children and raise them up to know and love You. You didn't make a mistake when You chose us to be their parents. Even though we have differences in the way we do that job, we pray that You will come alongside us and help us to become one in our parenting. Help us to listen to one another and be open-minded. Transform our anger into peaceful and helpful responses with one another and toward our kids. We want our parenting to bring us together and glorify You! We pray this in Your Son's Name, Amen!"

CHAPTER 10

WHEN AN IDOL MAKES THREE IN YOUR MARRIAGE (AMBER)

$\mathscr{S}$o, this is what marriage is," I thought to myself as I sat on the couch in our new apartment. There I was, home since 3:30 P.M., eating my dinner alone while I waited for my workaholic husband to walk through our front door. It would be hours before I saw him. My dream of intimate dinners together as a couple was fading fast as it dawned on me that our first year of marriage wasn't meeting my expectations.

As a teacher, I had to be at work by 7:00 A.M., which meant we saw each other only briefly at the start of the day. The fact that he often didn't get home from work until 8:00 P.M. meant we had approximately two hours a day together—if I could keep my eyes open that long. My mind began to wander: "Why did I get married in the first place if I am never going to actually *be with my husband*?" My longing left me lonely.

This would be just the beginning of my triggers in our marriage. Our first baby was born two months after our one-year wedding anniversary. A baby with extreme colic and reflux. With my husband's long hours, I carried the weight of caring for our son, Oliver. Before he was born, I considered myself a capable woman, but this was a situation I had not bargained for. My usual confidence gave way to fear, confusion, and isolation. I was dealing with the most beautiful mess of a child I could imagine, seemingly on my own, and suddenly I felt more alone than I had when I was single.

My dream was to enjoy a shared life with my husband, one in which he met my needs and I met his. Except life actually happened. He felt the pressure of providing, and that meant long hours in the entertainment industry. He was doing his best, but that wasn't good enough for me. Romance dwindled, and if we went on a date, it was because I took the initiative. In my mind, we were like strangers. The bitterness and discontent began to take root. Instead of counting my blessings, all I could see were my barriers. Barriers to the happy life I expected. Loneliness permeated my life and anger soon followed. They say that love is blind, but my anger blinded me from seeing the potential in our relationship.

I felt disconnected for reasons I believed were beyond my control, but that wasn't really the truth. I wasn't lonely because my husband worked a lot. I was lonely because of my own sinful anger and thought processes. In those early months, and even years, I often became aloof and withdrawn. My anger simmered under my calm exterior. My unhealthy coping mechanism was to shut down. Though Guy was a wonderful father, I wanted him to pay for what I considered his lack of commitment to our marriage and attentiveness to me as his wife. I longed for true companionship, and I felt the void on a routine basis. My frustration and anger turned me into an idolater, though I didn't fully grasp that at the time. All I knew was that I was unhappy, and I thought it was *because of him*.

Martha Peace, in her book *The Excellent Wife: A Biblical Perspective*, puts it like this:

> "It is not wrong for a wife to desire intimacy with her husband unless she desires it so intensely that she sins if she cannot have it. Then her desire becomes idolatrous. In those cases, even if her husband attempts to be more open with her, she is likely to be disappointed no matter how hard he tries. He may give up trying and then her idolatrous desire for intimacy becomes even more intense."[10]

The Bible speaks strongly about idolatry, but this passage from Colossians 3:5 (ESV) is especially convicting: "Put to death therefore what is earthly in you: sexual immorality, impurity, passion, evil desire, and covetousness, which is idolatry." Yep, I was coveting, alright! I coveted the ideal marriage. God wants our whole hearts to be devoted to Him, and when we put any thing or person before Him, we make it into an idol. My need and desire to change my husband became the thing that dictated my emotions and my joy. This intense craving colored my view of him and blinded me to my blessings. Martha Peace was right. Even when my husband tried to make me happy, I couldn't see it because my anger and bitterness prevented me from seeing clearly.

My loneliness grew the more I felt sorry for myself. The self-pity multiplied my discontent. My discontent depressed my spirit. My depressed spirit stole my gratitude. My lack of gratitude made me impossible to placate. My poor husband couldn't please me if he wanted to, because his efforts always fell short of my standards. I wanted him to fix the past, believing that was the only way to be happy in the future.

And so, my intimacy idol *almost* ruined us.

Because I was a Christ-follower, the Holy Spirit began to convict me. It was clear that Guy and I were unwitting hostages on a train that was hurling toward a ravine. If I didn't put the brakes on my wayward anger issues, then we were going to plummet into the depths of brokenness and take our son with us. We vowed never to divorce, but the prospect of living like strangers, or worse—enemies under one roof—seemed more than I could bear. I was willing to sacrifice my own happiness for the sake of my child, but as a Christ-follower, I knew our fractured relationship wasn't pleasing God. I didn't want to just get through it. I wanted our relationship to be great!

But how could I get my husband to be the provider, leader, spiritual giant, romantic, and friend that I thought I was getting when I married him? I tried, but I couldn't change him. Nagging him relentlessly didn't work. Yelling failed miserably. Trying to simply avoid conflict was impossible. *I had to change me.* I had to open my heart to a Holy Spirit transformation. I was called to love my husband, no matter what—just as Christ loved me when I was yet a sinner. I was called to love my husband, even if he never changed. Even if things got worse. My ability to fulfill my role as an excellent wife had nothing to do with my husband's performance. Yes, he could make it easier or harder on me, but ultimately, my goal was to honor God with *my* thoughts and actions. That is where the true and lasting joy would come from, not from an ideal husband.

Through times of quietness before the Lord, I sensed that the root of my anger and bitterness was pride. I wanted what I wanted the way I wanted it in the time frame I wanted it, otherwise I was miserable. That was idolatry. The Lord was speaking to my heart as I read my Bible every day. He encouraged me to lay down my own desires and to trust Him for my happiness. Gently, He revealed my selfishness. Kindly, He drew me to repentance. Slowly, He defused my anger and frustration. Tenderly, He asked me if I would be willing to bear fruit, even if my husband did not. Lovingly, He assured me that He would help me.

Yes, marriage was designed for intimacy. God desires for couples to love one another deeply, and to be a beautiful testimony of His love for the Church, but He never intended for any earthly relationship to replace Him as the center of our joy. My road to marital redemption started with humility and gratitude. Removing my idolatry of intimacy and desire to have my needs met by my husband required that I take my eyes off my own desires and place them on the only one who can truly meet my needs—the Lord.

The next practical thing I did was to make a list of all the things about my husband I was grateful for. If you, too, have an intimacy idol in your marriage, I encourage you to do the same. I didn't "feel" very grateful at first. It meant going against my feelings, using self-control, and thinking only thoughts that would edify my husband. It required trading wallowing with worshiping. Every time I felt bitter or hurt toward my husband, I took that trigger toward anger as a signal to turn to the Lord and thank Him for my marriage. That wasn't easy! But it was right. I certainly wasn't burying my head in the sand; I just knew that I needed to let the Holy Spirit work on my own heart before I could ever confront my husband in a loving and biblical way about his.

Transformation took time. Not much changed externally at first. I would have been hard-pressed to verbalize positive affirmations to Guy, as I was still healing from my pain, but if I was going to bless my husband and reposition God back into His rightful place as Lord over my life, then renewing my mind was paramount. Romans 12:2 (NET) says, "Do not be conformed to this present world, but be transformed by the renewing of your mind, so that you may test and approve what is the will of God— what is good and well-pleasing and perfect."

And you know what? The more I changed, the more Guy did too. He began to take his spiritual walk more seriously and we became more like-minded. When I got out of the way, the Holy Spirit had room to work on my husband. Eventually, he started studying the Bible and praying with me. He grew in generosity and was careful about how he spoke to me. He even sacrificed his prestigious and fulfilling job for another career that we hoped would allow better hours so he could be more fully present as a husband and father.

Today, people look at us and think we have always had a blissful marriage, but the truth is we worked hard, and we went through deep valleys to get to where we are now. God refined us both and we are still a work in progress. It's foundational to know and understand that the idol of a perfect marriage will prevent you from coming close to the biblical blessing of a healthy relationship. As you read this chapter, you may have a husband or wife who is not meeting your God-given needs or desires. Your wife may be downright rude and self-centered. Your husband may never know the deepest parts of your heart in the way you dreamed. She may struggle with respecting you. He may have a problem with procrastination. That is between your spouse and God. Your happiness and

When I got out of the way, the Holy Spirit had room to work on my husband.

joy will never be satisfied by any earthly possession, position, or person. It will only well up from the heart-spring of a man or woman whose hope is in Christ alone. If your need for intimacy with your husband or wife is an idol, tear it down today. Sacrifice your self-pity on the altar of gratitude. Pray this Psalm from the depths of your heart to God:

"Whom have I in heaven but you? And earth has nothing I desire besides you. My flesh and my heart may fail, but God is the strength of my heart and my portion forever." (Psalm 73:25–26, NIV)

Surrender your troubled marriage by giving it back to God. Your idol may not be for intimacy, but if your marriage or happiness is an idol in any way, and you are sinning as a result, then it's time to look at your heart. The idol of intimacy is a cold substitute for a husband or wife of any kind. And it can't compare to the One True God. Psalm 40:4 (NIV) says, "Blessed is the one who trusts in the Lord, who does not look to the proud, to those who turn aside to false gods." Humble yourself and put on a robe of gratitude today. The beautiful by-product can also be a healed marriage. At the very least it will lead to a healed *you*. I know from personal experience that idols make three a crowd, but there is always room for Christ at the center of your marriage. Make the trade today, and the intimacy from your relationship with the true Husband, Jesus Christ, will bless you in supernatural ways and bring you lasting joy.

> *The idol of intimacy is a cold substitute for a husband or wife of any kind. And it can't compare to the One True God.*

Let's Pray: "God, You are irreplaceable. Forgive me for placing the idol of intimacy with my spouse in Your rightful place.

MARRIAGE TRIGGERS

I know that my longings for a happy and healthy marriage are not wrong, but when I want that so much that I sin, then I am guilty of idolatry. Thank You, God, for being slow to anger and for being merciful to me. I surrender my husband/wife to You to convict and to grow toward spiritual growth. Be Lord of my life! Help me to focus on my love relationship with You so that my thoughts, words, and actions overflow from a heart that is content with You. In Jesus' Name, Amen."

CHAPTER 11

WHEN SEX IS MISSING FROM YOUR MARRIAGE (AMBER)

*G*rowing up in Christian circles, Gretchen heard the same old clichés about the needs and responsibilities of men and women in marriage. One in particular stood out: Men want sex all the time, but women don't. Little did she realize, this simply isn't true. Women were designed to experience pleasure as much as men. When she married her husband, Brian, she discovered that her sex drive was much higher than his. Because she believed that men were supposed to be the ones who wanted to make love as often as possible, her confidence and excitement over her status as a new wife plummeted. "What's wrong with me?" she wondered. "Is my husband not attracted to me?" Every time that Gretchen was in the mood for physical intimacy, she felt hesitant to ask Brian, and eventually, their sex life became stagnant. They both became angry and frustrated. The lack of connection, feelings of self-consciousness, and disparity between their needs was creating the wrong kind of sparks in their marriage.

Sometimes, the reasons for lack of intimacy in marriage aren't so obvious. Physical limitations, illness, depression, conflicting schedules, the responsibilities of child rearing, embarrassment and self-consciousness, or general apathy in the relationship are all common reasons for neglecting sex in marriage, but we may not be aware of them at first. We simply slip into a sexless marriage, unable to determine why. One of the main points that Guy and I hope you take away from reading *Marriage Triggers* is that great marriages don't just happen. They take intentionality. The same is true when it comes to your sex life. More on that in a moment, but first, let's look at what Scripture says on this sensitive topic. The Bible establishes that God designed us to enjoy sex in marriage:

"Do not deprive each other except perhaps by mutual consent and for a time, so that you may devote yourselves to prayer. Then come together again so that Satan will not tempt you because of your lack of self-control." (1 Corinthians 7:5 NIV)

"And the man and his wife were both naked and were not ashamed." (Genesis 2:25, ESV)

"And God blessed them. And God said to them, 'Be fruitful and multiply and fill the earth . . .'" (Genesis 1:28 ESV)

"Let him kiss me with the kisses of his mouth! For your love is better than wine." (Song of Solomon 1:2, ESV)

"Let your fountain be blessed, and rejoice in the wife of your youth, a lovely deer, a graceful doe. Let her breasts fill you at all times with delight; be intoxicated always in her love." (Proverbs 5:18–19, ESV)

Instead of becoming angry and frustrated, allowing walls to be constructed around your heart, Guy and I want to encourage those of you in a marriage where sex is infrequent or absent to begin with a conversation about this important aspect of your relationship. Take time to pray before you come together and approach the conversation with the goal of making progress, even small steps, toward intimacy. The point of making love is for connection and mutual pleasure. As in every area of the Christian life, that means we need to put on selflessness, understanding, empathy, and a willingness to bless our spouse. Pray that God will help you navigate these conversations. Be willing to act, even if it feels awkward or stilted at first, and remember that your sensitivity toward your husband or wife will go a long way in creating both romance and passion for one another.

Consider what speaker and author of *The Good Girl's Guide to Great Sex*, Sheila Wray Gregoire, shares about our attitudes when discussing differing libidos in marriage:

> "So, if you're in a marriage where you have a major libido difference, don't look at your spouse and say, 'if only he would grow up and stop being so shallow!' or 'if only she would reach out and stop being so frigid.' Don't look at your spouse at all. Instead, look at God. And ask Him to help you become more Christlike.... Simply be willing to make the efforts needed to enjoy making love with your spouse . . .
>
> "Our response to this problem must always be to look at God, not to try to change our spouse. Nowhere in Scripture does it say that we should demand our rights if we're not getting what we deserve. That's why 'Do not deprive' should never be used as a weapon; it goes against everything Scripture is for. Scripture focuses on servanthood, not on tyranny.
>
> "But nowhere in Scripture does it say that we can use God's word to justify ourselves so that we don't need to change, either." [11]

As you begin to work toward intimacy in your relationship, don't allow anger to fester. It may take time for your spouse to come around. Be patient with your spouse! God is compassionate and long-suffering toward us. Putting on those qualities goes a long way to foster loving feelings that can actually help you both feel more willing to engage in the sexual act. Anger will only continue to hinder that progress. The issue of sex being withheld or neglected in marriage is simply not discussed as openly in Christian circles as infidelity. This is not to say that we should demand sex, force ourselves on our spouses, or behave in any other inappropriate ways. Our priority should be the satisfaction of both partners, seeking to love and bless our husbands or wives. Sex should be mutual, tender, enjoyable, and exciting! If your attitude has been one of apathy or downright avoidance, then we urge you to take it seriously.

Guy and I have experienced, firsthand, that when our physical relationship is healthy, many of our other triggers toward anger fade. Our sex lives can actually be a proactive force against the temptation toward unrighteous anger in our marriages! The closeness we achieve through making sex a priority is a buffer against Satan's attempts to tempt us toward anger and distance in our relationship. God warns us not to let anything tear us apart as a couple— and that includes our sex lives. Marital sex feeds our need for love, and our love feeds our need for sex.

There are many wonderful resources available from Christian authors, like Gregoire, who can offer both specific tips for understanding the physiologi-

Our sex lives can actually be a proactive force against the temptation toward unrighteous anger in our marriages!

Marital sex feeds our need for love, and our love feeds our need for sex.

cal aspects of sex and suggestions for fostering an atmosphere for intimacy, and even scheduling sex so it becomes a priority. We often make plans to prepare meals for the week, but we don't give it a second thought to put plans in place to create the mood for making love with our spouses.

Because God places a high value on our sex lives, we need to too. Even if your sex life isn't fraught with problems, there may be room for improvement. Make the time and effort to prioritize sex, not because you feel you have to, but because you desire to experience the very best of all that your marriage has to offer.

Let's Pray: "God, I know You designed sex for our pleasure. I want to honor my spouse's needs and I want to feel that he/she honors mine. Lord, would You open my heart to creating a healthier sex life with my husband/wife. Help me to have the courage to initiate sex, to show my spouse that I love and desire him/her, and give me the wisdom to implement actions that will lead to intimacy. If we need to see a counselor or a doctor, Lord, lead us to the right people. Forgive me for neglecting this area of our marriage! As we come together physically, allow our sex life to remove the anger and frustrations we feel toward one another. In Jesus' Name, Amen!"

CHAPTER 12

WHEN YOU OR YOUR SPOUSE IS SICK OR INJURED (GUY)

*M*arriage brings with it the hope and excitement of amazing adventures. Plans to build a family, create a home, and experience the joys of life swirl around in our heads in the days leading up to our wedding ceremonies. Even though we vowed to love one another "in sickness and in health," some of us got a lot more than we bargained for. Some of us made plans to blend our lives together, move to a new city, or even switch careers to accommodate our loved one, but we didn't plan for a future where we find ourselves taking care of an unwell spouse.

Years ago, I struck up a candid conversation with a mom at a park who shared her struggle with anger over this difficult circumstance. Her list of grievances against her husband was longer than she cared to admit. She knew in her mind that it wasn't his fault that he was sick, but the resentment was hard to combat. Her husband injured his back on the job three years prior, so following numerous surgeries, weekly therapy, and countless doctor's appointments, his inability to do even the most basic work around the house compounded. There seemed no end in sight to her burdens. The couple had two young and active boys who needed attention, too, and the mom found herself on duty 24/7. The stress and pressure were taking a toll on their marriage. Anger commingled with her feelings of guilt. She admitted her embarrassment over the anger that bubbled up, sometimes out of nowhere. She took her marriage vows very seriously, to love her husband "in sickness and in health," but the reality held a much deeper meaning for their relationship than she'd expected.

Marriage is refining, isn't it? I don't think any of us blame that mom for her feelings. We have deep sympathy for her and her husband. For any of us in a situation where relief seems far away, God lovingly and gently calls us to dig deeper than we think we can. We can tune our ears to detect the truth, even as lies about what we are truly capable of echo in our ears. The promises of God were given to us for such times as these:

"Be strong and courageous. Do not be afraid or terrified because of them, for the Lord your God goes with you; he will never leave you nor forsake you . . . Do not be afraid; do not be discouraged." (Deuteronomy 31:6, 8, NIV)

God's charge to the Israelites as they prepared to cross the Jordan River is one we can take to heart. The Lord does not want us to live in fear, even when we face the illness of a loved one. He does not want us to fear the future. The Lord will carry us when the burdens we carry overwhelm us. He wants us to take one day at a time, leaning on Him to be present as our strength when we feel weak and trusting His plan for our marriage, even when it seems too hard.

The subject of caring for a sick spouse is personal for me. Shortly after college I moved to Houston, Texas, to take a job as an emergency medical technician (EMT) for a home health company while pursuing a career as a physician's assistant.

While in Houston, I envisioned working a few months in the field before moving into a sales position, but I soon found myself with a truckload of hospital beds, oxygen machines, suction devices, and shower potties! It was humbling. I thought the company was going to offer me a lucrative sales job, but it turned out that I was the guy they sent to handle hospice patients. Every day, I was face-to-face with husbands and wives, moms, dads, and kids who were in their last few months of life.

My first few patients ended up being my most memorable and impactful. The first was a man who had aggressive cancer. He was self-deprecating and funny, with a slang that my West Coast ears had never heard before. He was also resigned to the fact that he was going to be facing his last few months alone because his wife of many years simply couldn't face his illness. She'd shut down, unable to give her husband the care and attention he needed. I ended up being the one to pick up groceries for him in between

> *We can tune our ears to detect the truth, even as lies about what we are truly capable of echo in our ears.*

the frequent trips I made to his home to replace tubes and oxygen tanks. He passed away shortly afterward. While I was sympathetic toward both the husband and wife, I couldn't help but compare their relationship to another couple I attended to.

Bob was a former NASA engineer who had been battling brain cancer. What I witnessed between him and his wife, Monica, was an outpouring of love. His wife of thirty-plus years was his primary caregiver and she was such a blessing, not just to him, but to me as well. Monica had little concern for her own needs. She poured all that she had into caring for Bob and making him comfortable. Bob had the hope of Heaven as he approached the end of his life, but Monica lived out the love of Heaven as she cared for him, tenderly and sacrificially. She lived out her vows with grace and devotion. Their loving example made a strong impression on me.

A few months after Bob's passing, my own father, whom I was close to, passed away unexpectedly. I had to return to San Diego to help my mother and our family tie up loose ends. I barely had time to process the shock of his death when just thirty days after my father's passing, my mother suffered a massive stroke, leaving her incapacitated and wheelchair bound. Because my mom had no way to care for herself, and my father was no longer around to care for her, the responsibility fell to me. I spent the next two years taking care of her every need. My extended family was supportive, too, but I was the one who moved into a tiny double-wide trailer to feed, bathe, and comfort my mother. My inspiration was a combination of my love for my mom and dad, my faith, and a call to serve, as well as the incredible example of my patients in Houston. In retrospect, I see that God was preparing me to put on a selfless attitude when tragedy struck my own family.

The impact of taking care of my mother was life altering. I was a twenty-two-year-old kid, recently out of college and looking forward to my own future. I was caring for my mom and not a spouse, but with my father gone, I became the man of the house and the dynamics were very similar. I wish I could say it was smooth sailing, but I gained sixty pounds, and had trouble sleeping. Yet I kept putting one foot in front of the other. I spent a lot of alone time with my mother and felt extremely isolated and lonely during those years. I understand how anger can develop and how discontent can feel oppressive. Even so, I felt a devotion to my mother and a calling from the Lord to be sacrificial in my love and care for her. I could not have done so without the Lord's strength to carry me through. It became a conscious choice to choose joy and trust in God's plans for my life.

My mom's care eventually became more than I could handle. She enjoyed her life, limited as it was, in care facilities for several decades before joining my father in Heaven just a few years ago. Her joyful spirit helped my own. Not once did I hear my mother complain about her condition. Amber says that my mom is the best example she has ever seen of suffering well. Her paralyzed legs didn't stop her from "dancing" in her wheelchair. She looked forward to her weekly hair appointments and participated in Toastmasters, making jokes and being cheeky. Mom loved her kids and grandkids, delighting in regular visits and giving them rides on her wheels. And every weekend, you could find her singing her heart out at church services held in her building. She made the most of her life when most people would have faded into obscurity. I'll never forget her example of trusting the Lord, even when it hurts.

When Amber and I said our vows, "in sickness" meant something to me.

There are numerous verses in the Bible that speak to this need for strength, grace, and hope in the midst of difficult times. Perhaps you are in need of that encouragement. Consider these passages:

"Do not be anxious about anything, but in everything by prayer and supplication with thanksgiving let your requests be made known to God. And the peace of God, which surpasses all understanding, will guard your hearts and your minds in Christ Jesus." (Philippians 4:6–7, ESV)

"My grace is sufficient for you, for my power is made perfect in weakness." (2 Corinthians 12:9, ESV)

"God is our refuge and strength, an ever-present help in trouble. Therefore we will not fear." (Psalm 46:1–2, NIV)

As these verses illustrate, we have options for how we handle our triggers. I never thought my call to love and serve my family "in sickness and in health" would come so early. But when I found myself at the bottom, I also found God there to lift me up with His promises to love and honor me, to hear my prayer requests, to bless me in ways that only self-sacrifice can provide. I could have stewed in anger toward God or thrown a miserable pity party. Dealing with a sick spouse requires heavy lifting. Enduring injury or illness is never easy. But adding anger to the mix removes the opportunity to grow spiritually and to bond with our loved one in ways that represent what our wedding vows were made for. "I do," we said. When we or our spouses are sick or injured, that is the time to prove that we meant it.

Let's Pray: "Lord, I'm weary and worn. I'm angry too. Fear and frustration, hurt and helplessness often surround my heart and mind. I want to fulfill every aspect of my wedding vows to my spouse. I don't want to be angry anymore or feel resentful. Lord, help me to find joy in serving my spouse and joy in the life you have allowed me to live, even when I feel sick or am in pain. Help us to make the most of our marriage, even in sickness! Father, I invite You to help me think about my circumstances from a godly perspective. Equip me to offer gentle biblical responses to my spouse and comfort our hearts. In Jesus' Name, Amen!"

CHAPTER 13

WHEN YOUR ROLES
ARE NOT DEFINED (AMBER)

I couldn't wait to get married, have kids, and quit my job. Raised in a traditional home where my father worked long hours so my mom could stay home with me and my brother, just as their parents had done before them, I had no desire to buck the system. While Guy and I are now partners in both business and our home life, early on in our marriage these traditional roles suited me just fine.

Guy had a working mom and dad whose roles were different from the ones I saw growing up. In our marriage, the issue of equality in marriage and how to decide who does what and when has not been a trigger like it is for many couples. Even though Guy worked outside the home and I spent my days raising our boys, we felt like equals in every way. As soon as Guy came home from work, he jumped in to give me a break, helped with after-dinner dishes, and gave the kids their bedtime baths. As opportunities came my way to begin writing and speaking, Guy was my biggest cheerleader.

But for those who are triggered by an imbalance in marriage, you are not alone. In fact, I hear from readers about this trigger more than any other. And it's not just in Christian circles. My secular friends struggle to find equality in their marriages too. I wrestled with writing this chapter because Guy and I both long for this book to be balanced, not point fingers at husbands or wives, and offer both gentle conviction and hopeful encouragement to both parties, equally.

But this chapter will be a little different, only because the trigger itself largely stems from an overarching societal issue that permeates our thinking about gender, femininity versus masculinity, and our roles in marriage. Hang with me to the end, and trust that my heart is free of malice. I desire only to shed light on a touchy issue that I feel compelled to address despite my fears that it could be misconstrued or feel judgmental.

Let me just say for the record, gentlemen, I'm not against you. I'm for you! And ladies, I'm sympathetic to your need to feel like an equal. Please keep an open mind as we head into the rest of this chapter.

My friend Cali recently called me, sharing some happy news. She and her husband, Ben, were in counseling and they were finally making headway toward happiness after nearly ten years of marriage. What was it that caused her such elation? Cali had been furiously working to finish her daughter's costume for the school play later that night. Other tasks, like making an early dinner for the rest of the family, had to wait. But this time, Ben did something totally out of the ordinary. He offered to help Cali get dinner going while she stitched the final seams of angel wings. It was a first. You see, Ben was of the mind-set that women were the ones to serve the men. And that is true. Wives should serve their husbands. But it's only true because all of us are called to serve one another. Mark 10:44–45 (ESV) says, "And whoever would be first among you must be slave of all. For even the Son of Man came not to be served but to serve, and to give his life as a ransom for many."

Offering to help his wife with a household chore was not in Ben's habit. Cali was in a marriage with a good man who loved God and loved her, but his idea of his leadership role in marriage set him up as the provider and protector, Cali the attendant to his needs and the nurturer of their children. Without even realizing it, Ben's chauvinism manifested itself in subtle ways, not overtly such as by physically abusing his wife, but inadvertently by devaluing her as worthy of his service to her. Jesus didn't just make dinner for people—he continually fed the thousands, healed the discarded women of his society, and urged the early church to care for widows.

Maybe the above scenario surprises you. It doesn't surprise me. For Cali, the subtle messages of her lack of value to her husband are directly connected to how loved she feels. If husbands don't value their wives and serve them like Jesus did, then they don't love their wives like Jesus did:

"Husbands, love your wives, just as Christ loved the church and gave himself up for her." (Ephesians 5:25, NIV)

If your spouse doesn't feel loved, that's a big problem. Jesus' love was directly linked to His service and willingness to give Himself up for his Bride, the church.

The burden of this issue is not all on the Bens of the world. Whenever attitudes or actions in any believer are unbiblical, we are called upon to lovingly confront and communicate with them so as to win them over for Christ. Biblical confrontation is an area that needs growth within the Christian community at

Jesus' love was directly linked to His service and willingness to give Himself up for his Bride, the church.

large. Time and time again, women who feel "less than" in their marriages suffer silently, unwilling to engage in confrontation out of fear or intimidation. Their hearts become broken, resigned, embittered. As the old saying goes, what you permit, you promote, and what you allow will continue. Though the source of the issue may not be your fault, you have the responsibility, out of love for your husband, to broach the subject and get help if needed. Wives need to do the heart work prayerfully, seeking the Lord so that their communication with their husbands is respectful and full of loving-kindness, despite their hurt feelings—*especially when there are hurt feelings!* Men need to be humble, open to considering that this truly might be a sin issue in their lives and willing to take steps toward working through this trigger with grace and understanding.

I don't think any of us can deny that the feminist movement has done a lot of good in advocating for the basic human rights of women in recent decades, but we are in need of a biblical feminism. Biblical feminism seeks to esteem women as Jesus did, not offering lip service about equality but living it out among the sexes. Author Wendy Alsup speaks to this issue in her article in *Christianity Today*:

> "Gloria Steinem famously said a feminist is 'anyone who recognizes the equality and full humanity of women and men.' Is God then a feminist by her definition? If feminism in its purest sense is the quest for justice and equal rights for women, then, yes, God was the first feminist. God created woman in his image and bestowed on her equal dignity with man."[12]

Let's dig into this a bit more. Religion at large has been condemned throughout history because of its treatment of women. Women have suffered greatly because of their gender, but when Jesus came to earth, He dignified women, valuing them in ways that were radical and deemed inappropriate to the culture around Him. The devaluing of women at that time was deplorable. Treated as second-class citizens, women suffered at the hands of men. Jesus was revolutionary when He spoke to a Samaritan woman at the well, beckoned children to be cradled in His masculine arms, and graciously accepted Mary Magdalene's tearful adoration as she cleaned His feet with her hair though religious leaders scorned her checkered past. Jesus' actions reveal the heart of a God Man who came to both serve and esteem all mankind.

The traditional roles we often fall into are not wrong in and of themselves, but when these roles foster attitudes and treatment of women that are sinful and oppressive in nature, or overlook the dignity of women, we are in trouble and so are our marriages. We may have come a long way to elevate women, but we are still intrinsically tied to the past. Our society is valuing women more and more, but the Church, who should be the forerunners in this area just as Jesus was, is lagging. This leaves women feeling hurt, unable to trust or rely on church leadership to correct this wrong in our lifetime.

There are two key considerations when we talk about roles in marriage: leadership and gender differences.

LEADERSHIP

Guy and I often hear of husbands who view their leadership in marriage as a position of control. God describes leadership as a position for servanthood. Paul speaks of the hierarchy within the family: "But I want you to realize that the head of every man is Christ, and the head of the woman is man, and the head of Christ is God." (1 Corinthians 11:3, NIV)

This verse outlines the orderliness or hierarchy of leadership in the home. Leadership in marriage is not dictatorship or privilege. It is meant to bring an attitude of peace and fluency, not oppressive intimidation. God is our ultimate authority and He has the prerogative to structure our relationships, which He does with our good in mind. God has placed husbands as leaders over their wives. Wives are called to "come up under" their husband's authority. Guy's authority in our home does not cause me to feel threatened or subdued. He bears no "I'm in charge" attitude. His role has no greater value than mine. Rather, his confident authority is for my good, and I know it. Because Guy has a servant's heart and is sensitive to helping me fulfill my calling and my dreams, his leadership brings me no angst. Instead, he serves me in such a way that I can be the helper that God designed me to be as his wife. I feel more valued in his eyes because I am a woman, not the other way around. Whether male or female, if we jockey for leadership in a controlling manner or resist God-given authority because of a power struggle, we are not living out the example of Jesus' lifestyle of servanthood or His biblical design for marriage.

Perhaps your marriage looks different from mine and you feel pained by your husband's leadership approach. Ask the Lord to work in his heart and prayerfully consider a heart-to-heart conversation about this trigger. Because this issue can stem from long-held ideologies, this may be an area where you will need outside counsel. Trust that the Lord will help you to become unified and equal partners that love and respect one another as God designed.

FEMININITY VERSUS MASCULINITY

So where did we go wrong? Why is it that so many Christian men still tend to portray, sometimes unwittingly, a tone of superiority over women? One of the contributors to this widespread mentality could be a misunderstanding about our gender roles.

Practically speaking, we get into trouble when we confuse God's design for order in our marriage with cultural norms for femininity and masculinity. This is the moment of truth for couples who are battling angry reactions due to unbiblical or unequal roles in their relationship—or who no longer want to adhere to those roles.

Some couples do blossom and thrive from traditional roles of men being the breadwinner and women staying home to raise children, but more and more women feel triggered by these constraints and the attitudes that often accompany them. Our current social constructs are not always derived from Scripture; they are often derived from society. If this is true, then questioning why we think the way we do, especially if our perspectives are causing anger in our marriages, is critical.

If a woman wants to play football or a man pursues a career as a ballet dancer, we should not be discouraging such things as they relate to the Bible. If we adhere closely to societal norms that can be oppressive in nature, then we are not responding biblically to the men and women in our lives when they no longer feel comfortable with traditional roles. Historically, women have suffered the brunt of this way of thinking. While the playing field is beginning to level, it is a slow progress. The church body should be the first to challenge the status quo when there is unrighteous oppression and basic human rights are deprived simply because of one's gender. Human trafficking and slavery have received much attention, as has the recent #MeToo movement in Hollywood. The church has risen to the occasion as long as it pertains to a movement that doesn't hit close to home, but as soon as we begin to examine how similar issues are harming our marriages, we often dismiss them. We may say we agree with these bigger issues, but in our homes, the lines become blurry.

In Genesis 1:27 we read that God made male and female in His image. That means that God embodies both masculine and feminine qualities. Adam was made in God's likeness. Eve was also made in God's likeness. Our world needs both the masculine and feminine touch. But even subtly suggesting that one is better than the other is not biblical.

When a couple yields to God's design for leadership in marriage and also grasps that cultural norms are nonrestrictive as to how they relate to one another, then they are ahead of the curve. They are free to enjoy God's distinction of male leadership in the home as the husband serves his wife in humility, and wives are free to pursue anything that God calls them to without it being deemed unloving or neglectful. We realize that this may make some couples uncomfortable as they begin to prayerfully reevaluate their roles in marriage, but Jesus often stretches us beyond our comfort zones. If we truly believe that men and women are equal and desire to follow God's design for order in marriage, we will stop allowing culture to dictate our relationships or roles and embrace the freedom of biblical leadership in our homes. Husbands will esteem women as being better than themselves and that will be evidenced in their service to their wives, and wives will begin to speak up for what is right in a way that honors God and their husbands. And just maybe, we who are in Christian marriages will be as revolutionary as Jesus intended us to be.

Let's Pray: "Lord God, You are a God of order and creativity. You desire for men to be a loving authority in the home and for women to come up under that authority respectfully and in freedom, but our world has twisted and tainted Your good design. Help me to embrace my God-given role and to love my husband/wife unconditionally. Keep me and my husband/wife from buying into the world's ideals for marriage and breathe life into our relationship. Lord, if I have been in error by trying to control my husband/wife in ways that do not reflect my faith, show me and forgive me. Help us to define our roles in ways that show our love for one another and not because that's the way it's always been done. Help us to communicate kindly and graciously and heal the hurt that our angry reactions have caused. In Jesus' Name, Amen!"

CHAPTER 14

WHEN YOUR SPOUSE IS HAVING AN EMOTIONAL AFFAIR (AMBER)

*M*y ex-boyfriend kept writing to me every couple of years. Each time, I hit the Delete button. When Facebook came along, he sent me friend requests until I blocked him. After all, he was married. *I was married.* And we had history. Truthfully, there was no temptation on my part to connect with him—the relationship we had years ago was one God spared me from. Eventually, others came back into my life via social media, too—one or two former boyfriends from my past. It seemed harmless to connect, and yet the Holy Spirit kept nudging my heart that this was not a good idea.

Over the years, I have had the sad opportunity to offer counsel and encouragement to friends, family, and readers who have given in to the seemingly innocent temptation of corresponding with and even meeting up with people who are a direct threat to the covenant of their marriage vows. Very few of them sought out an affair. Each was lured in by the idea that their marriage was not enough. They wondered if they were missing out on something better. None of them turned away before it was too late.

Guy and I would both say our relationship's greatest strength is trust. I have no concern that he would be unfaithful to me, and vice versa. We recognize that we have enough trouble without inviting any measure of infidelity into the mix. During times of struggle in our marriage, it concerned me when I started to wonder about those past relationships and, although I knew that I was committed to my husband, the very thought of peering into the current lives of old flames seemed dangerous. So, I listened to the warning in my spirit and unfriended them.

I'm wondering about you. Do you think that just because you live far away from an ex or someone new you are chatting with online, they pose no threat? Do you justify the fact that you are drawn to your coworker simply because you have a mutual interest in your work? My pastor, Dudley Rutherford of Shepherd of the Hills Church in Porter Ranch, California, recently said, "It is the sharing of souls that creates soul mates." Affairs are not only physical. They are also *emotional.* Anything that comes between the oneness of body or heart of you and your spouse is counter to Scripture. As husband and wife, you are no longer two, but one:

"For this reason, a man will leave his father and his mother, and be united to his wife; and they shall become one flesh." (Genesis 2:24, BSB)

God doesn't take the marriage union lightly, and we shouldn't either. Those seemingly light moments when your heart is drawn to another are heavy burdens in disguise. How can we tell if we are starting down a slippery slope or heading toward the cliff? Take a moment to honestly ask yourself these questions:

1. Is my marriage currently having difficulties?
2. Do I sometimes think about what my exes or past flames are doing or if they still think about me?

3. Have I reached out to them with the intention of receiving some form of flattery or affirmation?

4. Do I check their Facebook pages on a regular basis?

5. Am I doing this secretly and keeping it from my spouse?

6. Would my spouse be upset if he/she knew I was connected to them or talking to them?

7. Do I daydream about what life with them would be like now instead of the one I am living with my spouse?

8. Does the thought of unfriending my ex cause me emotional pain?

If you answered "yes" to any of these questions or if you felt a check in your spirit as you read them, I would strongly urge you to let these people go—emotionally, relationally, physically, professionally, and mentally. This may seem extreme for some of you, but the truth is that when you play with fire, you can expect to get burned. When it comes to your marriage, no protection that can save your relationship is too extreme.

If you are entertaining any hint of impropriety with someone else, your marriage won't be the only relationship to suffer. Your children will be devastated. You will most likely lose friendships. In-law relationships will be damaged. In some cases, it will force you into or out of the workplace. One thing is certain: The illusion you have that this extramarital relationship is what you have been missing out on is simply that, an illusion. It is a wildfire, ready to devour you. It's not worth it. God warns us that our enemy is cunning and active. He says in 1 Peter 5:8 (NASB),

> *When it comes to your marriage, no protection that can save your relationship is too extreme.*

"Be of sober spirit, be on the alert. Your adversary, the devil, prowls around like a roaring lion, seeking someone to devour."

Jesus makes a comparison in Mark 9:43 (NIV), telling us to take our sin seriously: "If your hand causes you to stumble, cut it off. It is better for you to enter life maimed than with two hands to go into hell, where the fire never goes out." Those are strong words. Surely, we could also then say if your Facebook friendship with a former romantic interest causes you to stumble, you should cut it off too. Some of you need to hear it plainly: If you keep telling yourself that the communications are innocent, they are probably anything but. God doesn't mince words about adultery. Matthew 5:28 (NIV) says, "But I say, anyone who even looks at a woman with lust has already committed adultery with her in his heart."

In October of 2014, my friend Samantha learned this truth the hard way. Her emotional affair led to legal trouble and a ripple effect in her life that she never saw coming. She wrote:

"It all began with a phone call from an old boyfriend who reached out to me 23 years after he crushed and dismantled my heart. I had no idea what he wanted or why he called, but I immediately began justifying the contact by convincing myself that he was going to make amends like some sort of step in an AA program and I was going to help him by forgiving him or better yet, if he hadn't yet found Jesus, I was going to be the one to help him find Him. I missed the mark by not effectively communicating my needs to my husband. One of the hardest lessons I've learned is no one sets out in marriage with the goal of intentionally hurting their spouse. Emotional affairs happen when there is a wound or unfulfilled need not being met. This unhealed wound or unfulfilled need creates vulnerability, and where there is vulnerability there can be an entrance for the enemy to come in and establish ungodly soul ties. This is what happened to me. When you are in the eye of the storm, during sin and deception, it is nearly impossible to see clearly."

Samantha takes full responsibility for her actions, but the devastation of her emotional affair is palpable in the words of her husband, Max:

"Unfortunately, in situations like this, covering up the truth is common, which inevitably leads to mistrust. The truly painful aspect of the weeks that followed was not just being upset but feeling like I was an outsider to my own wife. I was made to feel like the bad guy for 'interfering' with what had occurred. Initially, the other person was defended and protected, not me. Samantha did not want to immediately and completely cut off this relationship, which I honestly could not understand. This was by far the most damaging part to me emotionally. It led me to bring the topic up a few times after several months had passed, which then instigated new issues because I could not just drop it and move on after the act of forgiving had occurred. She had cut most of it off, and reassured me she'd learned her lesson, but in my mind, any contact was still playing with fire. I believe there is a valuable lesson in our testimony that if either spouse has a lingering issue, then by definition you *both* have an issue that needs to be worked together, not just individually. Now in our eleventh year of marriage we have started Christian counseling, partly to help fully heal my wounds from way back when, and partly for improving communication skills and relational patterns."

It's been six years since Max and Samantha faced this life-changing moment in their marriage. While emotional affairs are not easily overcome, there is hope for couples who are dealing with anger and mistrust. Max's example of restoring their marriage is one filled with hope:

"Samantha has been through the wringer and has felt extremely disappointed in herself, I know. For that I love her, and it shows a high level of commitment and courage too. Time does help heal wounds. However, there are certain types of situations, every now and then, when thoughts of this situation get triggered and resurface. It makes me uncomfortable. I know through God's plan for marriage if we choose to work together as a threefold cord (Ecclesiastes 4:12, NIV) that we can withstand absolutely anything. In fact, in the end things like this will only make us stronger. That is what is best about the Christian life: there is always hope and strength even in the worst of situations. To me that is incredibly exciting and what marriage is all about."

The many layers of pain that couples have to sort through because of emotional affairs can be avoided. The temptation to find satisfaction with anyone outside of your marriage is an opportunity for your own marriage to improve if you are wise enough to do what is right. What's more important to you: honoring your vows and protecting your testimony as a Christ-follower, or this online relationship? Discipline yourself to use social media for good—it's not about doing what is right because it's easy; it's about doing what is right because it honors God. As a Christ-follower, your happiness is not the ultimate goal. But if you think your happiness depends on doing what is wrong, you will instead ensure unimaginable pain.

I'm thankful that my own marriage is stronger than it has ever been before, but it's not by accident. Guy and I have spent the last fourteen years building that trust with one another, and no other relationship is worth jeopardizing our unity. It wasn't worth it when things were tough, and it's not worth it now.

For those of you who have already engaged in an emotional affair, I hope you will also take Max's words to heart. It doesn't have to be the end of your marriage. Many couples have come through the fire, refined. Better. Stronger. 1 John 1:9 (NLT) says, "If we confess our sins, he is faithful and just to forgive us our sins and to cleanse us from all unrighteousness." There is no better moment than right now to release the heavy burden of an emotional affair. God promises to forgive you.

If you are the spouse who has been victimized by an emotional affair, forgiveness is not optional for you. Ephesians 4:32 (ESV) says, "Be kind to one another, tenderhearted, forgiving one another, as God in Christ forgave you." Like Max and Samantha, you may need time and godly counsel to sort out your confusion, rebuild trust, and establish a healthy relationship once again, but that should always be our hope and prayer. Jesus paid for the punishment of all our sins on the cross. We don't need to keep punishing our spouses over the sins of their past. Releasing our anger and pain frees us to heal and opens up the possibility of creating beauty from ashes.

Fanning an old flame will only create a wildfire that you can't control. Go ahead. Unfriend that past boyfriend or girlfriend and focus on the one you vowed before God to love on your wedding day. Get a new job, immediately, if necessary. Find a new church or move to a new town. Be open and communicate with your husband or wife about the state of your heart. Seek counseling and do what is right. And in so doing, you will extinguish the possibility for disaster in your life and the lives of your loved ones. *Unfriended equals protected*, and that's an action worth taking every time.

Let's Pray: "Heavenly Father, protect my marriage from any emotional or extramarital affair. Keep me from temptation. Keep my husband/wife from temptation. Give me the sensitivity to be honest and discerning in all my relationships outside of my marriage. Father, give me the courage to always do what is right. Rekindle the flames of love within the confines of my relationship with my spouse and let us not be deceived that we can play with fire and not get burned. Lord, forgive me for any inappropriate emotional ties I have made. Cleanse me and mold me into a husband/wife of integrity. Allow us both to be trustworthy and true. Help me to forgive as You have forgiven me, Lord. In Jesus' Name, Amen!"

CHAPTER 15

WHEN THERE IS NO SPIRITUAL LEADER (GUY)

O ne of the fondest memories I have from childhood is waking early, dropping out of my bed, and lumbering to the living room, where I would catch a glimpse of my mom sitting on the couch, her massive Bible resting in her lap. What a great image to have stuck in my memory! Quickly, the Bible would be shut and I would happily snuggle up in her lap. My father, on the other hand, was not a big reader, and he liked to wake every morning to a cup of coffee and a hot shower, where he would eventually play out passionate conversations—usually arguments with the morning radio broadcast from behind the closed bathroom door. As soon as I knocked, the radio turned off, the door opened, and out from behind a cloud of shower steam, my dad would emerge with the fresh scent of Aqua Velva and a smile, followed by a bear hug.

My mom and dad were as different as the way they started their mornings, but they shared the same passion for important things like my sister and me, our community, and our nation, as well as our family's faith. Without question, Sunday mornings meant church! We spent the morning getting dressed in our Sunday best—I even had to wear a suit from time to time depending on what we were doing after church. Usually, I went to my Sunday school class with all the other kids, but on suit days, I joined Mom and Dad in the pews of the main sanctuary, singing songs from the hymnals, trying to catch a glimpse of Pastor Domini through the forest of adults' legs.

I also got to witness another scene that has poignant meaning to me today: my dad in his happy place, serving the church as a greeter and usher, passing the offering plates and then cleaning up afterward. Dad was full of joyful pride while serving his church. Everyone knew him, and most got hugs whether they were huggers or not. And if there was a new face in the crowd, Dad was the first to shake a hand and make the person feel welcomed.

Even at that young age, I recognized that faith looks as different as the angle of every smile it inspires. I understood that Mom loved the Lord because she started every day focused on her Bible reading. I saw joy in my father when he was serving. Dad didn't write notes to hang on the bathroom mirror with Bible verses, and he didn't actively have us memorize Scripture verses and recite them back on special Bible nights. Dad didn't formally speak Scripture into our hearts. Instead, he directed our hearts through acts of love, a spirit of pure joy, and a level of trust in his Lord and Savior that spoke volumes.

The godly image I remember of my dad will stay with me forever: the self-sacrificial servant at home, at church, and in the community, the hardworking provider, the protector of our family, and the warmest, most friendly man I have ever known. These qualities came naturally to him. The Holy Spirit was alive and well in the heart of my father. His faith was not flashy or overt, but he led us spiritually according to his unique personality. Dad lived out James 2:26 (NIV): "As the body without the spirit is dead, so faith without deeds is dead."

Just like the morning vision of my mother and father, the expectations of spiritual leadership in Christian homes today are as numerous and unique as the households themselves. Expectations can be either healthy or a hindrance. And oftentimes, our own ideas about spiritual leadership in the home are influenced the most by what we witnessed from our own parents.

The Bible, however, promises us guidance to address this potential trigger even if that example was missing in our upbringing. God is wildly in love with us, and so we flourish under His care. Take a look at Zephaniah 3:17 (ESV): "The Lord your God . . . will rejoice over you with gladness; he will quiet you by his love; he will exult over you with loud singing." This is a relationship that is clearly not about dictatorship or misery. The Lord of Lords need not lord over us with a negative approach. He is the Lord because He is good, and He is for us. So should every husband emulate this kind of spiritual leadership in the home, fostering a mutual love and respect with his wife.

Often couples begin to stagnate spiritually because they aren't sure how to navigate spiritual leadership issues and they don't lovingly communicate with each other to discuss their individual expectations. Unfortunately, most of these conflicts are triggered when one spouse's view of spiritual leadership is different from the other spouse's. Judgmental words and frustration fly; personal attacks and deep disappointment lead to hardened hearts. Often, a husband is leading in his unique way, but his wife may not realize it or appreciate it. And sometimes, a husband is intimidated by his wife's spiritual muscles, which can cause him to shut down for fear of not making the grade. I don't recall my mother ever saying to my father, "I wish you did more to spiritually lead our kids." She never seemed frustrated that she was the only one who was reading the Bible, and she never questioned my father's faith.

Over the last few years, many husbands have shared with me their wives' frustrations that they seldom if ever "lead" spiritually, they don't initiate spiritual discussions, and they infrequently encourage their kids to grow in spiritual ways. My own wife has expressed some of this same frustration with me over the years, especially in the beginning of our marriage when she entered into a different picture than she'd imagined. Among a few of the images I broke for her, "the organized, well-studied, and motivated Bible-teacher dad" was certainly one of the greatest. We had countless conversations where she expressed her need for me to step up in that way and lead formal time with the kids, but try as I might, I had a difficult time reaching beyond myself to lead in the way she pictured.

Amber grew up having Scripture poured into her all week long. She was raised in a Bible-focused church, where they attended three nights a week and the kids recited verses in front of the congregation each Sunday. She attended Christian schools all the way through earning her master's degree, and she passionately reads the Bible cover to cover every year. It is a beautiful thing to watch your wife read, study, and share with such dedication, passion, and love. But this also made me feel . . . *less than.* Like I could never be on her spiritual level, which created great doubt in my role as the leader of my family and caused me to say things like, "How can I possibly teach her anything she doesn't already know?" "What can I possibly teach my kiddos in a way they will understand at this young age?" "Where do I even start?" I got so worked up about my inability to "lead" my family spiritually in the way she needed that I shut down. Meanwhile, I was growing spiritually, but in my own way, just as Amber embraced her knack for doing Bible study with our kids and let go of her resentment that this was not my strength.

And then one day, I got this great text message from Amber: "You are an excellent spiritual leader in our family, and I love you." She sent me a link to a blog post from author Sheila Wray Gregoire. She writes:

> "I'm not sure why we believe that the husband must be the stronger believer. He simply sets the tone for the family and is responsible for the family. It does not mean that if you have memorized more Scripture than he has that your family is somehow out of God's design. It doesn't mean that if you know the Bible better than he does that your family is violating God's code. Why do we always think that?"

Gregoire goes on to say:

> "People all relate to God in different ways. Some will read their Bible for 45 minutes a day and pray for 30, with multiple journals and coloring pencils on hand. I have a male friend who's a trucker, and he doesn't read his Bible that much. But he spends his days listening to the teaching programs on the Christian radio stations as he drives. I have other friends who like to hike in the woods and talk to God, or men who like to get their hands dirty and go and help

out the people in the congregation who need to move, or need their oil changed. Not everyone is a 'sit down and read your Bible and pray an in-depth prayer' kind of Christian. And I really do think that's okay. Don't get me wrong; I think Scripture is very important. But let's not assume that our own particular favorite way of relating to God is the 'right' one, and so our husbands should get in front of us and do what we do naturally, but then ramp it up a little bit. That's a stretch."[13]

When Amber and I finally embraced our different spiritual approaches, everything improved. Bitterness melted. Confidence soared. God tells us to "consider how we may spur one another on toward love and good deeds" in Hebrews 10:24 (NIV). Longing for our spouse to fulfill a specific idea of spiritual leadership is waste of our energy. Rather, let us put more time into considering the words and actions that will propel our husbands and wives to do the good work God has prepared them to do. Be your spouse's spiritual cheerleader, not his or her spiritual critic.

Perhaps your husband is an outdoorsman who shows his family the awe and wonder of God in creation on weekly hikes or paddleboarding with your kids at a nearby lake. Maybe your wife has a strength in leading your children in understanding the history of the Prophets in the Old Testament. When husbands and wives can celebrate and embrace one another's spiritual personalities, they come closer to connecting in the oneness that marriage was created for. Spiri-

> *Be your spouse's spiritual cheerleader, not his or her spiritual critic.*

Spiritual leadership is not a competition or a one-size-fits-all standard to live by.

tual leadership is not a competition or a one-size-fits-all standard to live by. Embrace one another's God-given strengths and unique traits and ask the Lord to guide you spiritually. Following His lead will never steer you wrong.

Let's Pray: "Father, You want us to be a home that flourishes spiritually. Thank You for making us different. Thank You for leading us with unconditional love and wisdom. Help us to see one another through Your eyes. Give us generous hearts and minds that honor You and build one another up. Help us to spur one another on toward love and good deeds—and help us to recognize that effort in one another! Break down destructive expectations and heal hurts and pain. Draw us together in unity as You designed our marriage to be. In Jesus' Name, Amen."

CHAPTER 16

WHEN YOUR SPOUSE IS DISHONEST (AMBER)

"Do you want to really live?
Would you love to live a long, happy life?
Then make sure you don't speak evil words
or use deceptive speech!" (Psalm 34:12–13, NET)

*H*e wanted to protect her. And himself. When Tracy discovered that her husband had been in a fender bender (again) and tried to cover it up, she was more than just triggered. She was infuriated.

Heather wanted to stop buying so many clothes, but she felt compelled to shop till she dropped. Hiding the bills from her husband felt harmless—until he started paying closer attention to their bank account.

For couples who struggle over dishonesty, anger mingles with mistrust. We can't dance around the issue. The problem with dishonesty is that it is outright sin, which inevitably erodes the very foundation of our relationships. And we all know what happens to the house built on sand.

The spouse who is lied to feels a series of unsavory emotions in addition to anger. Being lied to makes your spouse feel devalued, disrespected, and unloved. Mistrust floods the heart and mind. If

you yourself have a problem with honesty, it may seem fairly innocent, but to your spouse, it brings everything about your relationship into question. Spouses who have been lied to never know what
to believe. As the old saying goes, "One lie is enough to question all
truths." In the book of Proverbs, we see how things go for liars:

"A false witness will not go unpunished, and he who breathes
out lies will perish." (Proverbs 19:9, ESV)

And in Proverbs 26:28 (NLT), we read, "A lying tongue hates
its victims, and flattering words cause ruin."

Clearly, lying and a strong marriage are at odds with one another. How could anyone who desires to have a loving and fulfilling marriage consider lying to his or her spouse? Unfortunately,
it's part of human nature. Satan used deception in the garden with
Adam and Eve and they played into the cycle of deception, hiding,
shame, and excuses. They, too, felt innocent enough until the juice
dribbled down their chins and the shadowy chill of sin seeped into
their hearts. The very first couple in the Bible experienced suffering and loss because of the sinfulness of lying and deception—we
would do well, then, to take note and take truth telling seriously.

The purpose of our lives is to become like Jesus. When it
comes to lying, the scariest thought is that when we set out to
deceive our spouses in any way, we are behaving just like Satan:

"You are of your father the devil, and your will is to do your
father's desires. He was a murderer from the beginning, and does
not stand in the truth, because there is no truth in him. When
he lies, he speaks out of his own character, for he is a liar and the
father of lies." (John 8:44, ESV)

Lying is the bedfellow of fear. Spouses often lie to avoid trouble, not realizing that the solution to trouble is not in making
more of it by lying or attempting to cover something up. In order

to avoid pain or confrontation, we hide the truth, tell "little white lies," or tell half-truths. If we aren't willing to suffer for the sake of honesty, we are a long way from suffering for the sake of the cross. That should give us pause.

We don't always want to protect just ourselves. Sometimes, we lie so as not to hurt our spouses. We falsely believe that the pain of lying is less harmful than any sting the truth may inflict. We downplay the seriousness of the sin of lying and justify our actions. One psychotherapist suggests this approach to being honest in a situation where we fear the truth may hurt:

> "If you have to say something to your loved one that may be unsettling to him or her, I suggest you do it as gently as possible. 'Brutal honesty' has gotten a lot of press lately, but I have seen it do more damage than good. You need to present your issues with some degree of kindness. If not, your message may be buried in an avalanche of hurt feelings. You will both be much more able to communicate if your hearts are not wounded in the process."[14]

Biblically, we are called to seek out ways to be peacemakers, asking the Lord for wisdom and discernment. Our spouse's reaction to the truth is between him or her and the Lord, but being dishonest in order to spare our spouses from hurt feelings is not the answer.

In some marriages, both spouses are engaged in deceit. Fudging a little on taxes or agreeing to lie on an application for an apartment feel like they

If we aren't willing to suffer for the sake of honesty, we are a long way from suffering for the sake of the cross.

will do no harm. When couples cooperate with one another to lie, there are still consequences. Abram and Sarai are examples of this. As they traveled through Canaan, a severe famine hit the land. They decided to enter Egypt, but upon their arrival Abram cautioned Sarai to do him a favor by telling the officials that she was his sister. On account of Sarai's great beauty, he feared that the Egyptians would kill him and take her for themselves. The plan worked out just fine as Sarai was ushered into the palace and betrothed to the pharaoh while Abram was given his own royal treatment, until God's judgment fell on the people:

"But the Lord sent terrible plagues upon Pharaoh and his household because of Sarai, Abram's wife. So, Pharaoh summoned Abram and accused him sharply. 'What have you done to me?' he demanded. 'Why didn't you tell me she was your wife? Why did you say, "She is my sister," and allow me to take her as my wife? Now then, here is your wife. Take her and get out of here!' Pharaoh ordered some of his men to escort them, and he sent Abram out of the country, along with his wife and all his possessions." (Genesis 12:17–20, NLT)

Lying doesn't just impact our lives and the lives of our spouses. It often has a negative impact on others—just as the household of Pharaoh found out. Our dishonesty will always end in more widespread trouble than we bargained for. It is never, ever, worth it!

I think we can agree that lying for any reason is not justifiable for the Christ-follower. Even though we know it's natural, humanly speaking, to be dishonest, the good news is that we are not slaves to our human nature or to sin. Romans 6:6–7 (NLT) says, "We know that our old sinful selves were crucified with Christ so that sin might lose its power in our lives. We are no longer slaves to sin. For when we died with Christ, we were set free from the power of sin." God urges us to confess our sin to one another and to turn from our sinful ways. Coming clean is the biblical way to heal the wound of mistrust in our marriages.

But what about the spouse who is deeply affected by being lied to? I'd like to speak to you for a moment. I know that you feel angry and hurt, but I want you to carefully consider your own responses to your husband or wife. Please hear my heart here as I speak to you tenderly, and not in judgment. Are we more interested in punishing our spouse or doing what is right? It may be that you are still harboring resentment toward your spouse. I understand. How long will you punish your spouse for that? Creating a safe environment for honesty makes it that much easier for our spouses to tell us the truth. If we fly off the handle, berate our husbands for lying, or yell at our wives for misleading us, we are not displaying the kind of character we are demanding from our husbands or wives. That is the essence of hypocrisy. Their sin does not open the door for us to sin back.

Our biblical response to our lying spouses is to confront them in love, not in anger and frustration. I know that is not easy. But it is biblical, and it is right. Jeremiah 31:3 (NASB) reminds us of how God draws our own wayward hearts: "I have loved you with an everlasting love; Therefore, I have drawn you with lovingkindness." Meeting our spouses' sin with our love isn't just holy, it's hope-filled. Our loving-kindness mirrors the Lord Jesus to our spouses,

Creating a safe environment for honesty makes it that much easier for our spouses to tell us the truth.

and we get the opportunity to be the hands and feet of Jesus to them. If He is able to transform our hearts with his loving-kindness, drawing us to repentance, then extending that same loving-kindness to our husband or wife can be instrumental in transforming our marriages.

Lying brings only temporary and false security. It doesn't compare with a clean conscience. If you have not been telling the truth to your spouse, today is the day you get to begin. Honesty in marriage brings great comfort. It frees us to be ourselves and love one another in spite of our shortcomings. It's no small thing to offer grace to our spouses, working toward rebuilding trust without the complication of anger. Your husband or wife should be the person who accepts you and spurs you on toward love and good deeds, a safe harbor for any and every circumstance. The truth always sets us free. Your gentle and biblical responses will too.

Meeting our spouses' sin with our love isn't just holy, it's hope-filled.

> Let's Pray: "Father, You are truth and You highly value honesty in our lives. I know that You keep your promises and You say that when we confess our sins You will wash them away by Jesus' blood. Lord, for any form of dishonesty or sinful anger I have displayed toward my spouse, forgive me! Help me to be honest and unafraid. Remove my frustration and help me think clearly. Lord, we desire to have a marriage that is secure and healthy. Allow us to trust one another and to work hard to keep building that trust between us. Lord, if I need to let go of my fear that my spouse will be dishonest again, show me and help me! Draw us with loving-kindness and let that overflow in our marriage so that love can flourish again. Thank You, Lord! In Jesus' Name, Amen!"

SECTION TWO:

INTERNAL TRIGGERS

When the things that trigger us toward anger have everything to do with us . . .

Let's face it. Even our external triggers have a lot to do with us, don't they? In section one, we covered many of the things that set us off, but in section two, we will take a closer look at how we can take ownership of internal struggles that can trigger us—things like feeling misunderstood, personality clashes, and past wounds that are still festering. Please, continue this path with us toward gentle biblical responses. Prayerfully invite the Holy Spirit to speak to your heart, to heal your hurts, and to make your marriage all that He designed it to be!

CHAPTER 17

WHEN YOU FEEL MISUNDERSTOOD AND LONELY (AMBER)

Loneliness is a symptom of feeling unknown or misunder-stood. It's one thing to be single and lonely, but to be married and lonely can feel like a prison. We don't have to go very far into the Scriptures to see that one of God's first priorities from the beginning of creation was to solve the problem of Adam's loneli-ness in the Garden of Eden:

"Then the Lord God said, 'It is not good for the man to be alone. I will make a helper who is just right for him.'" (Genesis 2:18, NLT)

Because I waited much later than typical in life to be mar-ried, my expectations for companionship with my husband were high. I'd had enough of pulling my own weight. I longed for a shared life. I've already talked about the demanding schedules that Guy and I faced early in our marriage that often kept us physically apart, but even when we came together, we frequently felt a million miles away. I wasn't sure he really knew me—or ac-cepted me. Guy felt equally lost and disconnected. We certainly didn't relate to one another as lovers and I would have settled for friends, but in reality, we often felt like individuals performing duties in and around the home and in parenting our kids.

Well-meaning friends suggested we have more date nights, but with very young children, a strict budget that didn't allow for babysitters, and living in a small town without any family to help us, that idea felt overwhelming. If our marital success depended on date nights, we were in serious trouble! The feelings of disconnection triggered deep anxiety and stress in our relationship. I realized we were in peril when I began to ask myself, "What is the point of being married?" I hadn't said "I do" to a roommate relationship. I wanted a husband who cherished me in ways nobody ever had before.

Like many couples, when Guy and I felt unheard and unseen, we resorted to yelling, but that failed miserably. It's crazy to think that anyone who is being yelled at will suddenly have a light-bulb moment or be open-minded to whatever you are trying to convey. The only message a husband or wife hears when they are being yelled at is that their spouse does not respect them. It also reveals a sinful lack of self-control. Let me be blunt. If you or your spouse have a habit of raising your voice, you are doing far more harm than good. It needs to stop. Begin with this one discipline of taming your tongue. There were times when

> *The only message a husband or wife hears when they are being yelled at is that their spouse does not respect them.*

I physically had to bite my tongue as the Lord began to work on my heart in this area. Proverbs 29:11 (ESV) says, "A fool gives full vent to his spirit, but a wise man quietly holds it back." When you yell at one another, does it help or lead to more problems? Our husbands and wives will never see our better nature if we constantly show them our worst side. Our desire for every couple reading *Marriage Triggers* is that you will be open to what God would do in your marriage so that you can turn away from angry reactions—like yelling—and let the Holy Spirit shape gentle biblical responses in your hearts.

So, what might that look like, practically? I often tell parents who struggle with anger toward their kids that one of the first steps toward regaining control of our tempers is to take a "Holy Pause" and regain our composure. When you feel like you are going to explode as the result of any trigger, take a break. There is nothing our anger can do that love can't do better. Stepping away to breathe and calm our frazzled hearts makes room for us to then approach our spouse with loving-kindness, instead of saying things we will regret. Then come together, outside of a time

> *Our husbands and wives will never see our better nature if we constantly show them our worst side.*

of conflict, to listen in order to *understand*, instead of listening to *respond*. This obviously means that both husband and wife need to be open and willing to do the hard work toward progress. God has called us to reconciliation, so if you feel hardened against this idea, begin by asking God to soften your heart—or your spouse's heart! Maybe you and your spouse never raise your voices at one another, but take a moment to identify any other patterns of unhealthy communication and commit to seeking the Lord to help you find better ways of getting through to your spouse.

Every day of my life until 2005, I groped my way from my bed to my bathroom, being careful not to stub my toes. In fourth grade, my teacher saw me squinting to see the chalkboard. A

There is nothing our anger can do that love can't do better.

quick trip to the eye doctor confirmed her suspicion: I was nearsighted. After three years of wearing cumbersome glasses, my parents got me contact lenses, but nothing changed my life more than the day I went under the knife for Lasik eye surgery. The moment I sat up from the operating table, I could see without any assistance. If you were to ask me what was the best thing I have ever done for myself, I'd tell you it was this miraculous medical procedure. I could go swimming and open my eyes underwater now that the fear of losing a contact lens was gone. No more blurry walks to the kitchen for morning coffee. When Guy and I are having trouble understanding one another, or we are actively struggling to see each other's hearts, we need this kind of clarity. It's time for us to put on our "Jesus Glasses."

For me, it's a way of viewing my husband as God views Him and filtering what I see and hear from him through the eyes and ears of Jesus. I will literally pantomime putting these glasses on and it helps me shift my perspective, which can often be distorted by my own sin, personality differences, or agenda. Jesus Glasses replace negative thinking with believing the best about one another ... They're a spiritual Lasik surgery for the heart. Instead of jumping to conclusions or making mountains out of molehills, they soften our perspectives and help us be open to seeing our husband or wife for who they truly are. Even if what we see is a flawed person who is truly in the wrong, our responses won't stem from unrighteous anger, but from a desire to lovingly confront our spouse and repair our relationship, just as Jesus would do. If that means imagining Jesus Glasses in order to remind ourselves of what our attitudes should be as Christ-followers, then it's not beneath us to do it. Whatever it takes to give us eyes to see our spouses as Jesus does is worth it.

One of the biggest complaints I hear from women is that their husbands criticize them when there are dishes in the sink or the kids' laundry is not put away. For a woman who has been pulled in thousands of different directions, who has not had a minute to even go to the bathroom in peace and quiet, and who often feels overwhelmed by the constant and thankless cycle of wash, rinse, repeat in her daily life, that kind of criticism severs her heartstrings from her husband. When a husband makes it a point to see the countless "unseen" things his wife does around the home and verbalizes that to her, he is only helping himself. His wife feels appreciated and understood, and in turn is more willing to offer similar affirmations and respect to her husband.

When men come through the door from the workday, it's equally important to acknowledge the things they do that go unseen. Our husbands cross the thresholds of our homes, leaving behind an often antagonistic world. They don't need an antagonistic wife confronting them as they step into the house too. In general, it's good for both wives and husbands to examine how often what they say is critical, versus uplifting. Do our words breathe life into our husbands and wives more often than not? If that is a focus in our relationship, then it's likely we won't feel misunderstood or taken for granted for very long.

Men won't typically communicate this to their wives, but they can feel cast aside when kids come into the picture. Starting a family is a huge life change that few of us are prepared for. In most Christian homes, the child-rearing falls largely in the lap of the mother, and it's very easy to get caught up in the needs of children, neglecting to give the same kind of attention to our husbands. That can feel tremendously hurtful, even if husbands understand why it is happening. How often do moms plan fun things for the kids but rarely do so for their husbands? I am guilty of this. There are some ideas in Christian culture that I like to call "churchical" because they sound good, but they aren't truly biblical. I don't ascribe to the popular notion that we must put our spouses first, because biblically, the only pecking order we see in Scripture comes from Luke 10:27 (NIV):

"He answered, 'Love the Lord your God with all your heart and with all your soul and with all your strength and with all your mind'; and, 'Love your neighbor as yourself.'"

If we love God, and love others, then there is no need to create a hierarchy of affection in our homes. We are free to simply live out our Christian faith at the right time, in the right place, toward the right person. That said, if we are loving our husbands well, then we are not overlooking their desire to be seen, treated specially, and nurtured in ways that may not be equal in time but communicate our understanding of their needs and desires. And vice versa!

Some of the biggest arguments couples engage in are sparked by tone of voice and body language. It's easy to misread someone's intentions when we zero in on these modes of communication. This is where giving our spouse the benefit of the doubt is crucial. Not only can we misconstrue what our spouses are trying to communicate because we read them wrong, but we can also use our body language and tone of voice to drip with sarcasm or reveal what we are really thinking. Rolling our eyes, shaking our heads, and giving "looks that kill" are all weapons easily wielded when we are angry. Tone of voice and body language should be used to bless our husbands and wives and improve communication, not as manipulative tools that wound the one we promised to love and respect.

If tone of voice and body language are a continual problem for you as a couple, try this. As soon as you sense that the way your spouse is coming across to you is negative or hurtful, stop and take a breath. Instead of being quick to anger, say something like this: "Guy, I want to make sure I'm not hearing the wrong thing. The way you are talking to me sounds _____. Am I mistaken?" Take spouses at their word. If they say that is not how they meant to come across, then believe them. You can come together outside of conflict to express certain mannerisms or tones that are difficult for you to process, but do so in a spirit that desires to understand one another and work together to be sensitive to each other.

It's comforting to know that Jesus relates to our feelings of being misunderstood. In John chapter 1, it says:

"He was in the world, and the world was made through him, yet the world did not know him. He came to his own, and his own people did not receive him. But to all who did receive him, who believed in his name, he gave the right to become children of God, who were born, not of blood nor of the will of the flesh nor of the will of man, but of God." (John 1:10–13, ESV)

Jesus caused quite a stir when early in His ministry, He was performing miraculous healings and casting out demons. When His earthly brothers heard about it, they found where He was and tried to take Him away, saying, "He's out of his mind" (Mark 3:21, NLT). Imagine! Those who should have known Him best had no idea that He was the Son of God! Talk about being misunderstood! And yet, what was His response? He kept doing what was right and good, blessing others in the midst of His own often lonely path. Can we do the same? If we are passionate about truly living out our faith, then we must walk in His steps. Feeling unknown by our spouses is not an excuse to resort to our own sinful behaviors. We are called to something much higher than that—and much more holy.

Is your heart aching from feelings of loneliness? Do you wish that your wife or husband would finally see who you really are instead of viewing you through distorted lenses? Let us be like Jesus and not sin in our weakness. Never stop going to the throne, boldly, to receive His mercy and grace when you need it most. You and I may plead for our spouses to change their ways or put themselves in our shoes so that this trigger might be removed, but someone far greater has already given us the key to victory. He promises to give us exactly what we need, when we need it.

One more thought to consider when we are feeling lonely in our marriages: Loneliness is a result of our fallenness. When Adam and Eve sinned, they became separated from God. Because God is love, our disconnectedness from love naturally results in loneliness. Sin turns us inward on ourselves, an antithesis to connection and selflessness, which are attributes of love. Because marriage is a picture of God's love for us, we were never meant to be lonely in our husband-wife relationships. Adam and Eve's sinful decision to go outside of God's protective boundaries in the garden set the stage for every relationship under Heaven to be less than what God designed. Still, if we want to strengthen our marriages, we can't lose sight of the fact that God designed husbands and wives to love one another—and we can't fully realize that blessing if we are constantly feeling underappreciated and misunderstood. Ultimately, we can all remember that Jesus died for us, putting an end to the worst kind of loneliness—separation from God. Perhaps all of us would do well to think of ourselves less, identifying with Christ in His own lonely journey, seeking to view our husbands and wives as the gifts they are, and doing our best to tell them so.

Let's Pray: "Lord Jesus, You are our example of how to carry on when we feel lonely, misunderstood, or unknown. Thank You for continuing to do what was right, even when it cost You everything. I want to be a husband/wife who believes the best about my spouse. I desire to be intimately connected with him/her and to communicate my care and concern for his/ her heart. I want to encourage his/her heart, not be a source of heartbreak. Lord, You can bring us together and help us understand one another. Remove our anger and frustrations so we can breathe and begin anew. In Jesus' Name, Amen!"

CHAPTER 18

WHEN YOU ARE WEARY AND EXHAUSTED (AMBER)

*E*vangelist and author Luis Palau said, "When you face the perils of weariness, carelessness, and confusion, don't pray for an easier life. Pray instead to be a stronger man or woman of God."[15] Recently, I took a poll asking my community of readers if they feel triggered by weariness and exhaustion. My in-box flooded with comments. Men and women today are being pulled in a thousand directions, but it isn't just busy schedules that exhaust us. The emotional burdens of our responsibilities and the disappointments of life make us weary and worn. For most of us, the answer isn't fleeing to a deserted island to rest and recuperate or waving a wand and having all our problems vanish. It's much more along the lines of Luis Palau's wisdom.

Early on in our marriage, when Guy and I were first starting our family, we were idealistic and full of hope that by one another's side, life would become easier as a shared experience. But, during the first three years of marriage, we were faced with some of the top stressors that experts say lead to every manner of both health conditions and causes for marital conflicts.[16]

I was working and attending grad school full-time when my father was diagnosed with an inoperable benign brain tumor. Within months, Guy got a promotion at work with added responsibilities, we got married, and we moved into a new apartment to start our life together. Soon after that, we discovered I was pregnant. Suddenly, I was put on bed rest and unable to finish the teaching year or say good-bye to the students and colleagues whom I loved. I ended up quitting my teaching job when Oliver was born, while Guy took a new job in marketing. Within six months and with a colicky newborn in my life, I became a property manager working from home. Not long afterward we added another son to the mix, Guy was laid off from his new job due to the economic crisis, and we were forced to make a big move three hours north to a small town for yet another new job. Emotionally, it felt crushing. We were the poster children for stress and conflict. Many of you have endured similar burdens. This is the stuff of life. It makes us weary. Exhausted. Angry at the world and angry with each other.

Military families endure long separations. Parents of teenagers feel drained from negative and defiant arguments with their once compliant sons and daughters. Many couples I talk to are caring for sick children or elderly parents. It's not just our physical health that is jeopardized by all the exhaustion, weariness, and stress. Our marriages are so deeply buried under the weight of our cares that we become quick to anger and irritable, living with a short fuse. Simple things cause us to snap and raise our voices. Many of us feel victimized and on edge. These are the moments when we yell at our husbands for leaving dishes on the counter or spew foul language at our wives for making dinner plans without consulting us. Seemingly small things become the breaking point.

It's easy to put on a victim mentality in such circumstances, but doing the easy thing is rarely the Christ-like thing.

Our marriage triggers become marriage testers. They reveal what our relationship is really made of. The test of weariness and exhaustion makes or breaks us. For those of us in the middle of this weariness, there is hope. We find help to go from triggered to triumphant in 1 Peter 2:21 (ESV), where the apostle Peter guides us toward godly thinking. He writes:

"For to this you have been called, because Christ also suffered for you, leaving you an example, so that you might follow in his steps."

Christ is our example. That's a lot to aspire to, isn't it? Nevertheless, God doesn't give us an "out" in times of weariness and exhaustion. When Jesus was cursed, He blessed. When needy crowds pressed in relentlessly, He made Himself available. When they were hungry, He fed them. When they needed correction, He lovingly but boldly gave it to them. When they hurt Him, He forgave them. When they deserved punishment, He graced them. When He needed sleep, He pressed on. When His friends deserted Him, He had compassion for them. When He suffered, He kept the eternal picture in mind. *He kept you and me in mind.*

> *Our marriage triggers become marriage testers.*

On our wedding days, we promised to love and cherish our husbands and wives. In order to do that well, we can't just pull ourselves up by our bootstraps when the going gets rough. Allowing Jesus to care for us enables us to care for our spouses.

Matthew 11:28 (ERV) says, "Come to me all of you who are tired from the heavy burden you have been forced to carry. I will give you rest."

Your burdens may feel anything but light today. God is not trying to make light of your circumstances. He wants you to see your circumstances through His light. We are not helpless or forgotten in our times of need. Jesus knows the number of hairs on your head. Why would He take such care to count them if they were not precious to Him? If *you* were not precious to Him? Don't allow an hour to go by before taking your cares to Jesus. Because the Bible is our Daily Bread, we become malnourished spiritually if we neglect it. Spending time with the Lord refreshes our spirits and strengthens us to face both our trials and our triggers.

It's easy to think that the Lord has forgotten us when we feel worn-out by our heavy burdens. But the Lord can never forget us! Isaiah 49:16 (NIV) tells us our names are written on the palms of His hands! If you feel triggered by the weariness and exhaustion of your circumstances, you won't be able to combat your anger and frustration until you lay your burden down at the feet of Jesus. He wants to show us the way toward a peaceful life and a fulfilling marriage. He's ready to teach us how to be gentle and humble—and all we have to do is rest in His company. Jesus asks us to learn from Him. To take note of how gentle and humble He is. In the same way that our angry reactions typically spark even bigger angry reactions in our spouses, Jesus' gentle and humble spirit rubs off on us, producing a supernatural steadiness of heart and mind.

God is not trying to make light of your circumstances. He wants you to see your circumstances through His light.

As we give our weariness to the Lord, His gentleness becomes our gentleness. His humility is reflected in our own. Gentleness softens our body language and moderates our tone of voice.

Humility lets us look tenderly on the needs of one another. As we grow in character, exhaustion gives way to strength upon strength, equipping us with the ability to overcome the temptation to lash out in frustration.

Your circumstances may feel hopeless and the ache for relief may consume you. The book of Proverbs is filled with practical wisdom. The woman in chapter 31 is a hard worker whose life is filled with many responsibilities, and yet her relationship with her husband is healthy and pleasant. Both she and her husband are respected in their community. Proverbs 31:25 (NIV) describes her attitude despite the many people she manages and tasks in her day:

"She is clothed with strength and dignity; she can laugh at the days to come."

I wish I could say that I mirrored the example of the Proverbs 31 woman during the first intense years in our marriage, but I didn't. Her example shows us that angry reactions aren't our only option. We can put on "strength and dignity," allowing God to give us the ability to look forward to the days ahead—even laugh at them—instead of dreading them.

The husband and wife who are followers of Christ never have to operate on empty or be quick to anger. We are promised the fruit of supernatural strength and given an example in the person of Jesus Christ. Luis Palau suggests that we need to pray to become a stronger "man or woman of God" when we are weary.[17] Matthew reminds us that our strength is found in the gentleness and humility of Jesus. Proverbs shows us the image of a happy wife living a happy life because her faith, not her circumstances, dictates her joy.

How strong are you today? You can answer that by gauging

how gentle and humble you are toward your spouse. Though we imagine that pouring out in such a way may drain us further, the opposite is true. Our angry or sullen attitude is the real joy robber. The heart filled with godly character has very little room for angry reactions. Because we live in a fallen world where brokenness and the pressures of life are the norm, our days of exhaustion won't end until we are home in Heaven. Let's not waste these precious moments by being triggered. Instead, let's accept the invitation to "come" to the Lord and find rest for our souls by demonstrating gentleness and humility in our marriages as we, too, laugh at the days to come.

> *The heart filled with godly character has very little room for angry reactions.*

Let's Pray: "Lord Jesus, thank You for being an example to us. You hold the answer to all our marriage problems. You know how we feel. Thank You for inviting us to come. We beg of You to help us grow in gentleness and humility. Lord, give us a desire to put our husband's/wife's needs before our own. As we pour out, let us be filled supernaturally with Your rest. Give us a marriage that is stronger than we could have ever dreamed. Help us to laugh at the days to come and to delight in one another. Jesus, we rest in Your strength and we operate from a place of fullness and joy, even when circumstances threaten to drain us. Let us love one another deeply, letting go of anger and resentment. In Jesus' Name, Amen!"

CHAPTER 19

WHEN YOUR MARRIAGE EBBS AND FLOWS (AMBER)

*T*he Pacific Ocean is our backyard here in Southern California. Most weekends, the coastline teems with locals and tourists escaping the heat in exchange for the peaceful lull of ocean waves. The ebb and flow of the water is mesmerizing. Seasons in marriage ebb and flow in much the same way. Unfortunately, the waxing and waning of our personal relationships isn't always as harmonious as what we find in nature. For most couples, there is a natural progression of highs and lows in marriage, but the distance we sometimes feel can cause animosity and resentment, wedging even more distance between us. That isn't God's desire for us. Our marriage relationship should be the most consistent source of joy through all the inconsistent stages of life.

Not long ago, Guy and I enjoyed several months during which I felt we were closer than ever—a truly joyful season in our marriage—and then bam, suddenly, we felt a million miles apart. I suppose there are couples whose relationship remains steady on a consistent basis, but Guy and I have spent a good part of our marriage riding the waves of marital intimacy. I have a feeling you may be a lot like us. When the closeness you long to feel is absent, it's easy to get angry and frustrated. Instead of engaging our spouses in positive ways, we snap at one another, allow feelings of hopelessness to overshadow our thinking, or grow complacent as one day bleeds

> *Our marriage relationship should be the most consistent source of joy through all the inconsistent stages of life.*

into the next. I was tempted to say "why bother" during some of our hardest days. I didn't feel like I had the energy or strength to try harder. Had I yielded to these thoughts, I would have missed out on the most meaningful relationship of my life.

When couples grow distant, it's often due to several factors. As I sat back and thought through what had changed for us to cause such a discrepancy in our relationship, I realized that over the years, there have been several key contributing influences that impacted how close Guy and I felt toward one another. We aren't alone. As we continue to work with families who struggle with similar issues, some specific themes stand out. Here are some common reasons why feelings of closeness in marriage can ebb and flow:

Workloads
Life changes
Permissiveness of sin
Exhaustion
Spiritual warfare
Lack of intimacy
Busy schedules
Individual personal problems such as depression
Lack of spiritual growth

Hormonal and other physiological changes
Stress
Illness
Seasonal shifts
Comparing ourselves with others
Starting a family

Life happens. Some of the items from the above list are simply part of the ages and stages of our lives and we can't always do much about them, but spiritually speaking, we can glean from God's Word to draw our hearts back into loving communion with one another. God designed man and woman to be "united into one," according to Mark 10:8–9 (NLT), which continues: "Since they are no longer two but one, let no one split apart what God has joined together." Our hearts were meant to be knitted together in such a way that we take on a new and wonderful identity as a married couple.

Too often we allow circumstances and attitudes to separate us. God doesn't want us to settle for coexistence, being together in a physical sense but figuratively standing on two sides of a great emotional crevice. Yes, our relationships will ebb and flow, but as soon as we notice that we are drifting apart, we must be proactive to speak to one another's hearts and breathe life back into our marriages. If we let our anger *get* the best of us, we sabotage God's best *for* us.

> *If we let our anger GET the best of us, we sabotage God's best FOR us.*

Our human nature is lazy. It's far easier to let bygones be bygones or focus on more pleasant efforts, but that is not the mark of a passionate Christ-follower. Intimacy between husbands and wives is built, one loving selfless act, one thoughtful caring word at a time. There's much more at stake than an anger-filled marriage. Lazy spouses make for bad marriages. Bad marriages make for poor testimonies. Work hard to improve your marriage and be a light to the world.

The best-case scenario is that you and your spouse are reading this book together, both willing to set aside angry reactions for gentle biblical responses. But even if that is not the case, do not lose heart! Your ability to grow in affection does not have to depend on the reciprocal affection of your husband or wife. The thought of growing in intimacy seems impossible if only one spouse is willing to do the work, but don't undervalue the impact you can have on your husband or wife through your godly example. Time and time again, Guy has broken down my walls by his willingness to love me in ways I don't deserve. When he does that, he is treating me like Jesus does. The powerful force of a spouse willing to do what is right, simply because it is right, holds more sway than any of our defenses. Your spouse will often change when you love him or her in this way, but do not expect that. Love your spouse because your allegiance is with God, who loved you when you yourself were lost.

Lazy spouses make for bad marriages. Bad marriages make for poor testimonies.

In chapter 6, we talked at length about the power of prayer, but we want to drive home that prayer is foundational for healthy marriages. John 15:7 (NIV) says, "If you remain in me and my words remain in you, ask whatever you wish, and it will

Your ability to grow in affection does not have to depend on the reciprocal affection of your husband or wife.

be done for you." Does that mean that we can ask for absolutely anything and God will do it? Not quite. *The Quest Study Bible* offers some helpful clarification:

> "It is impossible to pray correctly apart from knowing and believing Jesus' teachings. As long as we remain in him and his words remain in us, our desires will be consistent with his will. Praying in [Jesus'] name (v. 16) refers to requests in line with who Jesus is and what will advance his work. Such prayers reflect total dependence on him."[18]

The closer we draw to the Lord, the more our prayer requests will be in line with God's will for our lives. But here's the thing. We already know that biblically, God wants our marriages to be filled with love and purpose. We know that God wants us to grow in the Fruit of the Spirit and bring Him glory. Asking the Lord to remove our angry reactions and resentment and make our marriages the best they can be is a prayer that God longs to answer. That should fill us with hope! Pray. Pray like your marriage depends on it! *Because it does.* We don't even have to *feel* like praying. We just need to be disciplined to pray. As we talk with the Lord about the desires of our hearts and grow our relationship with Him, the feelings follow—both for the Lord and for our spouses.

The powerful force of a spouse willing to do what is right, simply because it is right, holds more sway than any of our defenses.

Romance and deep connectedness is a beautiful God-given thing. Spiritually, something supernatural and full of wonder occurs when we give our hearts to our spouses. In the classic novel

Jane Eyre by Charlotte Brontë, the main character, Jane, falls impossibly in love with the master of Thornfield Hall, Mr. Rochester. As the governess, Jane is outclassed by her employer and yet, love finds a way. In a climactic scene in which Jane tells Mr. Rochester that she must seek new employment abroad, he says:

> "I have a strange feeling with regard to you. As if I had a string somewhere under my left ribs, tightly knotted to a similar string in you. And if you were to leave, I'm afraid that cord of communion would snap. And I have a notion that I'd take to bleeding inwardly."[19]

There is truth to his words. Some of us reading this chapter feel as if we, too, are bleeding inwardly. The string has snapped, and we feel the distance growing between us and our spouses even though they may very well be in the next room over, not an ocean away. We may be mad at our husbands or wives, but some of us may be just as angry with God. We didn't sign up to feel this way in our marriages. Whether your anger is directed toward your spouse or God, you'd best deal with it, here and now.

Applying Ephesians 4:26–27 (MSG) to our marriages allows us to be steady emotionally and spiritually: "Don't use your anger as fuel for revenge. And don't stay angry. Don't go to bed angry. Don't give the Devil that kind of foothold in your life."

When I first began to study what the Bible says about anger, this verse scared me. Allowing anger to fester for any reason can swing wide the door for Satan to waltz into our lives. Can you imagine? One of the most dangerous things we can do is to give him a "foothold" in our marriages. Do you and your spouse struggle with a marriage that ebbs and flows? Might that be because your anger has made Satan a third wheel? God is clear: Deal with your anger and deal with it directly. When you get in your bed at night, nothing, especially anger, should come between you and your spouse.

What's a good next step in rekindling the intimacy of our souls? Peter gives us a good place to start. He writes, "Turn away from evil and do good. Search for peace, and work to maintain it." (1 Peter 3:11, NLT) Pretty simple, isn't it? Open the front door and kick Satan to the curb by prayerfully dealing with your anger. Turn from evil. Do good. Don't just imagine a peaceful and loving home. Search out ways to become a peacemaker with your husband or wife. And then "work to maintain it" as much as it depends on you to do so. Wake up in the morning ready to breathe life into the heart of your husband or wife. Spontaneity is overrated. Make a plan to do and say specific things that you know will tighten the string from your heart to his/hers.

Wives, that might mean keeping your opinions to yourself about how long it has taken for your husband to fix the faucet. Husbands, that might mean wooing your wife again, like you did when you were dating. It might involve saying "I can overlook that" when little things your spouse does typically trigger you. It may mean speaking highly of your spouse to others. Or it could be that you commit to getting home an hour earlier every night. Or really listening when your spouse lovingly confronts you about sin in your life. Rekindling the closeness in your marriage may

> *Spontaneity is overrated. Make a plan to do and say specific things that you know will tighten the string from your heart to his/hers.*

require you to prioritize your responsibilities or to express your love to your spouse more often than not.

God, in His divine magnificence, holds the Earth and everything in it in the palms of His hands. The oceans of the world ebb and flow naturally, never receding too far from the shoreline and flowing back again like clockwork. Just as God created the seas, He created marriage to reflect His love and care for us, His children. Let's be intentional to communicate and connect with our husbands and wives as God intended. Some of us have spent far too long out to sea, and it's time to find safe harbor with our spouses once again.

Let's Pray: "Lord Jesus, You long to answer our prayers for a better marriage. Thank You for never leaving us or forsaking us. You see the distance that lies between me and my spouse. Draw our hearts together in ways they have never been connected before. Lord, I don't want to feel a world away from my husband/wife. Speak to his/her heart. Speak to mine! Soften our hearts and allow us to truly feel the affection we had for one another in the beginning of our relationship. Help us both to see one another with new eyes. Help us to put into practice both actions and words that will allow our love to blossom, and help us to get rid of any anger or resentment. We desire to honor You, Lord, for all You have done for us! In Jesus' Name, Amen!"

CHAPTER 20

WHEN YOU ARE NO LONGER FRIENDS (GUY)

*A*ccording to Dr. John Gottman, professor emeritus of psychology and the founder of the Gottman Institute, there are several things to consider when gauging the health of your marriage, such as respect, affection, and friendship. He defines friendship as liking each other—having fun and laughing together. Ask most singles to describe their ideal spouse and most will say without even thinking that they want to marry their best friend—that person that just gets us, accepts our warts, and is enjoyable to be around. We may start out in our relationships as friends, then transition to spouses and lovers, but many of us lose the friendships that drew us to our spouses in the first place. If our marriages are laced with anger, the chance for rekindling our friendship with our spouse is even further at risk.[20]

Whenever you face triggers in marriage, whatever the igniter, Amber and I hope you learn to deal with them instead of ignoring them or suffering as a result of them. We long for you to not just love, but *like* your spouse. There have been a few times in the aftermath of an argument when Amber has said to me, "I know you love me, but do you like me?" Her question pained me. How could we get to a place where she questioned if I even liked her?

The bond of friendship that we should be continuing to foster with our wives and husbands often takes a backseat to the business of life. Transitioning into a new home together, building careers, sharing bills and expenses from a joint bank account—the normal demands of everyday life, and eventually the big one that shifts everything, parenting—tend to push friendship aside as a priority. Don't let that happen! Decide, right here, to do whatever it takes to be each other's best friend.

Friendship isn't just about pleasing ourselves. It's a godly characteristic.

Jesus calls His disciples His friends: "No longer do I call you servants, for the servant does not know what his master is doing; but I have called you friends, for all that I have heard from my Father I have made known to you." (John 15:15, ESV)

God is called the friend of Abraham: "And the Scripture was fulfilled that says, 'Abraham believed God, and it was counted to him as righteousness'—and he was called a friend of God." (James 2:23, ESV)

Friendship reveals our respect for God: "He who withholds kindness from a friend forsakes the fear of the Almighty." (Job 6:14, ESV)

Friends help, benefit, and protect one another: "Two are better than one, because they have a good reward for their toil. For if they fall, one will lift up his fellow." (Ecclesiastes 4:9–10, ESV)

Friendship is a quality of love: "Greater love has no one than this, that someone lay down his life for his friends." (John 15:13, ESV)

Friendship strengthens our spirituality: "That is, that we may be mutually encouraged by each other's faith, both yours and mine." (Romans 1:12, ESV)

Friendship seeks the best for one another. A friend that "wounds" us (tells us the truth) is the best kind of friend: "Faithful are the wounds of a friend . . ." (Proverbs 27:6, KJV)

The Bible describes Jesus as our friend. Are you convinced that without a strong friendship in your marriage, you are both missing out on blessings and spiritually deprived? When anger is a central component of our relationship, we are neither revealing our best selves or inviting our spouses to be their best. Henry Ford said, "My best friend is the one who brings out the best in me." [21] Think back to the first time you met your spouse. What drew you to him or her? What quality about the person stood out to you? What was it about the time you spent together that you really enjoyed?

Now, think about what your daily lives involve today. Do you speak to each other differently? Are you excited to see each other after time apart? Do you want to give your spouse a call during the day or plan a date with him/her? When you see your spouse, do you smile? Does the thought of him/her irk you or impress you? And does your wife/husband bring out the best in you and vice versa?

The answers to these questions can be telling. As we shed light on this issue in your marriage, we want you to have hope! Friendship with your spouse is not a pipe dream, and Amber and I can testify to that. We wouldn't have called ourselves friends during certain periods of our own relationship, but now, we truly are one another's best friend. The first person we both want to share good news with is each other. If she needs someone to pray for her or lift her spirits, I'm her go-to person. When I have an opportunity to pick up a new hobby or some other fun escape, it's Amber who I want to experience those things with.

Just the other day, we were lamenting that we don't have many local friends in our everyday lives. Running our production company, writing books, homeschooling, and ministry needs don't leave a lot of room for making friends. We have felt the void and taken steps to try and connect with men and women in our church, but those connections haven't always come easily. Try as we may, BFFs have seemed to elude us. While we have dear friends that we speak to regularly, most of them live hours away or even across the country. As Amber and I talked about this issue, an important truth dawned on her: "There are seasons of life when girlfriends are hard to find. The Lord used these seasons to solidify my friendship with you, Babe. That's a good thing!" She was right. As we dealt with our triggers in marriage, we naturally became better friends, but God used a season where outside friendships were a challenge to bring us even closer together. God doesn't waste anything in our lives; even circumstances that seem pointless can be used for God to favor us in ways that we never expected.

I have a confession to make. This won't sound very spiritual, but Amber and I met in a hot tub. Yep, we did. We were on a ski trip at Mammoth Mountain with a large group of singles from our church, not realizing that we were about to meet our future husband/wife. At the time, I would have told you that I was done dating. I honestly thought it was just not in the cards for me to find my soul mate, and I was going to look at my single status as a blessing to refocus my life on giving my time and effort to others in need. Still, I was having a hard time convincing myself of that because I have always cherished the idea of being a dad and a husband, but dating, quite honestly, stunk! I believed I never had a chance with that beauty I met on the ski trip, and it took

Amber and me another year before we officially became friends. Within just a few months of that, I fell head over heels in love. And I wasted no time in telling her.

We were engaged, married, and expecting our first child in quick succession. Though we were obviously friendly for those few months leading up to our engagement, we honestly didn't develop a strong friendship. There is a difference. Our love for movie nights watching *Napoleon Dynamite* and eating home-made pizza was nice, but it wasn't very deep. We were caught up in lovey-dovey feelings instead. Our quick romance didn't give us much of a foundation of friendship to help us when the hard times hit. That took many years of trial and error. It would be through shared circumstances, difficult transitions, and eventually many wonderful blessings in work and family life for Amber and me to grow into true friends. There is now a sweet kindred connection that we had never experienced before.

Learning to enjoy one another even when you don't see eye to eye is key. You don't have to agree on everything to be great companions. If you don't have the friendship, here are a few things you can do to reestablish that connection:

1. Make a list of what made you friends in the first place. Keep that at the forefront of your mind.
2. Lighten the mood when you are together. Do whatever it takes. Tell dumb jokes or do something lighthearted. Amber and I recently went out for a cheap date night of miniature golf. At one particularly challenging hole, we laughed till we cried when it took me twenty-three swings to get my neon ball up a steep hill and around a curve. It did our hearts good!

3. Take several of the Bible verses from this chapter on friendship and commit them to memory. Turn them into prayers, asking the Holy Spirit to seal your friendship.

4. If you normally turn to a friend for advice or help, begin turning to your spouse first, instead.

5. Do things that you wish a friend would do for you. Be thoughtful. Offer to make dinner, send your spouse a note just because, or tell your spouse how talented you think he/she is.

The incredible Helen Keller said, "Walking with a friend in the dark is better than walking alone in the light."[22] I recognize that your marriage relationship may feel like it's passing through a dark period. Don't ever believe that walking alone in the light would be better for you. God did not make a mistake when He brought you and your husband or wife together. He gave you one another for the sake of love and for the blessing of friendship. To make a friend, you must be a friend. Your marriage is the best place to start.

To make a friend, you must be a friend.

Let's Pray: "Lord, I miss my friend, my wife/husband. We have grown apart and our anger has hardened our hearts. Help us to see each other as friends and to apply the truth from Your Word to our marriage. I long for companionship, Lord! Jesus, thank You for being a Friend to me at all times. I know I can count on You to give us ideas and creativity to help us build our bond with one another again. Thank You, Father, for the gift of my marriage. In Jesus' Name, Amen!"

CHAPTER 21

WHEN COMMUNICATION IS BROKEN
(AMBER)

*I*t was our first Christmas together and we had been married just shy of a year. Christmas Eve was spent alone, just the two of us, as we dined on prime rib and Yorkshire pudding. I was giddy with excitement and anticipation. Guy and I agreed to open stockings after dinner, and I couldn't wait to see what thoughtful gifts my husband had chosen for me. Guy urged me to go first, and I eagerly reached inside and pulled out a garish red feather boa flecked with sequins. While I thought that was odd, I wasn't prepared for the silly gag gifts and cheap dime-store gadgets that I opened, one after the other. Fighting back tears, I forced a smile, but Guy was no dummy. He easily read the look of confusion and disappointment on my face. His stocking was brimming with expensive cologne, movie theater tickets, and his favorite treats. It was one of those moments where our ideas of "fun" stocking items meant one thing to me and another thing to Guy.

The Christmas of 2006 wasn't the last time our communication broke down. Guy and I aren't the only ones who credit broken communication as one of our biggest triggers. Broken communication is a result of broken people. Understanding that opens our hearts to demonstrating grace toward our spouses. As much as I want to be the best wife I can be, I'm a sinner—and so is Guy. In those earlier years of our marriage, our angry reactions to conflict turned adversarial or hurtful. They should have been opportunities to learn about one another and grow in grace. Some of the biggest issues relating to poor communication include:

Bottling feelings instead of talking about them
Using a tone of voice that is angry or rude
Nagging
Ignoring
Passive-aggressive behavior
Being distracted by devices
Making assumptions
Feeling unheard
Not following through on agreements
Arguing to win instead of talking to problem-solve
Name-calling
Using foul language
Texting instead of talking
Hearing but not listening

It's enough to throw our hands up in the air in defeat. But don't despair—the Bible has the answers to all our communication triggers. No matter how challenging your specific communication issues are, there is always hope for improvement if both husband and wife are willing to try.

Broken communication is a result of broken people. Understanding that opens our hearts to demonstrating grace toward our spouses.

When we begin to take one another for granted or harp on our spouses, we are not treating each other as we would want to be treated. Matthew 7:12 (ESV) says, "So whatever you wish that others would do to you, do also to them, for this is the Law and the Proph-ets." Notice, the verse does not say we should yell, throw a fit, re-treat and sulk, or gossip to others about our husbands or wives. When Guy and I are in the middle of a disagreement, the Holy Spirit often enters my thinking and prompts my heart with this question: "Amber, do *you* want to win, or do you want *love* to win?"

When we live selflessly, we make a point to set down our phones, speak kindly, and listen intently. It matters to us how we come across to our husbands or wives. We long to know what they are thinking and to share our hearts mutually on deep lev-els. When both spouses take this attitude, love wins. Angry re-actions give way to gentle biblical responses. This requires that both partners be reasonable and express a caring attitude, even when they disagree on an issue.

It's not always what we *say* that causes issues. Broken com-munication can also come from what we *don't* say. My husband knows, because I have told him far too many times, that words of affirmation are my love language.[23] I feel most cared for when he compliments me. Most days, I could put on a brand-new outfit, dye my hair red (his favorite color), and he may or may not bat an eye. I've learned that all the nagging and complaining about my need for compliments don't get through to him. But guess what? It doesn't wound me anymore. I know my husband thinks

I'm beautiful and that he loves me. Occasionally he remembers to tell me. For all his areas of growth, he still can't seem to verbally express his admiration for me to the extent I would like. Our marriage improved when I let that go. For a long time, I held it against him. I reasoned that *if he loved me*, he'd communicate in my love language. Instead, I've learned that *if I loved him*, I'd accept him for who he is. Guy communicates his love and appreciation for me by doing the dishes, changing diapers, and surprising me with flowers. How sad for us both if I measured my husband's love and desire for me by whether he speaks my language. Be careful not to put too much stock into what your spouse *doesn't* say. Look for all the ways your spouse *does* communicate love and commitment to you.

We could spend the rest of this book going over examples of broken communication, but what will serve us best is to understand the root of the issue. Before we go any further, some of us have a choice to make. Are you willing to make your marriage better? Is there a desire within you to believe the best is yet to come? Will you allow the Holy Spirit to help you heal from broken communication? And are you open to putting some of these biblical insights into practice? If so, then you are positioned to reach the wonderful potential God has in store for your marriage.

A good foundational truth for healthy communication is found in Matthew 15:18 (NIV). The apostle writes, "But the things that come out of a person's mouth come from the heart, and these defile them." As much as we would like to point fingers and focus on how to fix our spouse, the truth of the matter is that we can only change ourselves. This verse reveals to us where broken communication begins: in our own hearts. The things we say, or don't say, flow from our hearts. Dark heart, dark words. Kind heart, kind words. Resentful heart, resentful words. Godly thinking, godly communication.

The only way for a heart to be transformed is by committing to reading our Bibles and applying what we read. I wish I could give you three easy things to say or do to guarantee perfect communication in your marriage, but the answer is that both husbands and wives need to have daily time in the Word of God and in prayer. When relationship triggers jostle us, whatever is in our hearts will spill out. If the Truths of God's Word, like Matthew 7:12, are deeply rooted in our hearts, then our natural responses turn *supernatural*. The only way we can breathe life into our spouses is if we are intentionally being transformed by the renewing of our minds through God's Word (Romans 12:2, NIV). By the time you read the last page of *Marriage Triggers*, it's our prayer that your marriage will be the best it has ever been because your relationship with Jesus is the best it has ever been.

When I was working on my struggle with anger in my parenting, I often took one or two verses that related directly to my specific trigger and simply read, prayed, and meditated on those few truths every day until I began to see a difference in my life. It changed everything! Take a moment to pray and ask God to soften your heart as you read the following Bible verses. Examples of some simple prayers that you can pray throughout the day follow each verse:

"Whoever keeps his mouth and his tongue keeps himself out of trouble." (Proverbs 21:23, ESV) *Lord, help me to "keep my mouth" from words that wound. I don't want trouble in my marriage because of my mouth.*

"A soft answer turns away wrath, but a harsh word stirs up anger." (Proverbs 15:1, ESV) *Father God, I don't want to stir up anger or make things worse when I speak to my wife/husband. Help me to speak softly and kindly, even if my spouse is not doing so.*

"Set a guard, O Lord, over my mouth; keep watch over the door of my lips!" (Psalm 141:3, ESV) *Jesus, in the heat of the moment, I have a hard time saying the right thing. Lord, guard my mouth so that I only speak life to my husband/wife!*

A great starting point for couples who have broken communication is to choose a verse or two from the above list and ask God to speak into your marriage with those verses in mind. Write them out and put them on display in your kitchen, on your bathroom mirror, or on the steering wheel of your car. Set a reminder on your phone with the communication goal you have in mind and the Bible verse you are dwelling on so that it pops up several times a day. We can't do and say the same old things and expect a different result. If communication breakdowns are constant triggers in your home, you have nothing to lose by focusing on these verses and asking God to do His work in your marriage.

> *When relationship triggers jostle us, whatever is in our hearts will spill out.*

It's hard to break old habits. Instead of being quick to anger and starting a yelling match with one another, Guy and I have learned to say, outside of times of conflict, "Babe, I have something on my mind. When is a good time for you in the next few days that we can take half an hour to chat?" When we do come together, our tone and demeanor make all the difference. We speak from a place of trying to solve a problem instead of speaking with an accusatory tone or with a desire to win an argument. We say things like, "Guy, I know there is a lot of stress lately with your work, but it sometimes feels like you are directing that toward me and speaking bluntly. It feels unkind. I'm betting you don't even realize it, but would you be willing to think about your tone of voice when you talk to me?" We even give each other permission to say things that make us stop in our tracks when we feel triggered. One of us will say, "Hey, Babe, can you say that a little differently?" or "Can we lighten up this conversation? I think we are going down a wrong path with our tone here." It's like a little white flag of surrender, allowing us both the chance to calm down and settle our emotions before we explode. Sometimes we simply say, "I'm not ready to talk. Can we discuss it after the kids go to school?" When two people are willing to communicate with honesty, patience, empathy, and grace, they experience the blessings of obeying God's commands—the blessings of a peaceful and loving marriage.

Not long ago, I heard from a friend of mine that her brother's marriage had ended. She told me that her former sister-in-law was a good person and such a delight to be around, but as soon as her brother entered the room, the sister-in-law visibly changed. Her demeanor, attitude, and body language became adversarial. Her warm personality turned icy. Just the presence of her husband caused her to bristle.

The communication breakdowns with your spouse may be so prolific that you feel trapped in negativity. Naturally, we don't think positively about our husband or wife when frustration mounts, but as Christ-followers we are not called to natural reactions. We are called to supernatural responses. Some of us may need to make attitude adjustments. Guy and I constantly work on checking ourselves to see if we are believing the best about one another. When you give your spouse the benefit of the doubt, you receive the benefits! Most likely, your husband or wife isn't a boogie monster out to get you. Your spouse simply doesn't know what is bothering you or how he/she is coming across. This is why taking the time to have focused conversations, even in busy seasons of life, is so important. We do well to give our spouses the benefit of the doubt. I'm able to respond gently to my husband when I remind myself that he is my teammate and partner, not just someone I feel at odds with.

Sadly, if spouses are unwilling to even attempt to change when an issue of broken communication is at hand, they are only hurting themselves. How unwise! If that describes your spouse, don't lose hope. We believe that the blessings of your own desire to do what is right will bring healing and strength to your marriage. As you do the right thing, the joy of the Lord, not your marriage, becomes your strength. Invest in living out God's instructions for yourself. Communicate the desires of your heart, trusting that with His help, better communication will take shape.

When Guy and I look back on that first Christmas together as husband and wife, we can't help but laugh. Nowadays, he knows the kinds of gifts I hope for in my stocking, but nothing compares to the gift of his willingness to communicate with me, openly and honestly. We urge you to be prayerful, to believe the best about one another, and to commit to communicating in ways that bring you together. A happy

When you give your spouse the benefit of the doubt, you receive the benefits!

marriage where communication thrives is a reward you can enjoy now, but the messages you send to one another supersede good communication. They convey your willingness to fulfill the eternal purpose of your life, to love God and to love others.

Let's Pray: "Dear Lord, you have given us instructions in Your Word so that we are not helpless to know how to talk with one another. My husband/wife and I are not communicating in ways that honor You. We feel stuck! Lord, I want to believe the best about my spouse, and I want him/her to believe the best about me. Father, please help us to communicate with loving-kindness. Let our hearts be so in tune with Your heart that our words, body language, tone of voice, and actions demonstrate our desire to communicate effectively. Father, I love my husband/wife. Do good work in our marriage, opening up our ability to talk with one another in ways that make us stronger, not tearing each other apart. In Jesus' Name, Amen!"

CHAPTER 22

WHEN ONE OF YOU NEEDS AN ATTITUDE ADJUSTMENT (AMBER)

*F*rames filled with newborn pictures rested next to our engagement and wedding portraits on the thick carpeting of our tiny apartment, a brief timeline of our new life together. Giddy as a schoolgirl, I loved working on projects around the house that made our little space *home*. On this particular weekend, finishing a few such projects was something I was eager to tackle. I spent weeks combing stores for frames that complemented one another, choosing sizes and styles that would suit our tastes. I turned on background music, set out the hammer and nails, and waited for Guy to join me. This wall of memories meant a lot to me. To him, not so much. That was obvious the moment he came around the corner, saw my layout, and sighed.

Immediately, I bristled. I couldn't understand why my husband had to "huff and puff" over things I thought should be fun and rewarding. All he had to do was nail them into place. I didn't just want him to participate, I wanted his attitude to be lighthearted and uplifting. In our early years as a married couple, it felt like he was stealing the joy from many of our interactions together. But it wasn't just Guy that needed an attitude adjustment. I rarely understood that our ideas of fun weren't always the same.

My husband is more laid-back than I am, and often he allows me to make plans and steer the ship. That part of our relationship worked well most of the time, but it also conditioned me to turn self-centered, assuming Guy would go along with whatever I decided we should do, whenever I wanted him to. And when he didn't, I wasn't very empathetic or accommodating. Our attitudes triggered angry arguments and often left both of us sulking or licking our wounds. It tasted bitter and left us thirsty for something better.

It took quite a few years for us to learn to communicate clearly, looking out for the interests of one another without becoming resentful. One day, I was having my quiet time reading my Bible when a series of verses that I had read many times before spoke to my heart in a fresh way as I considered my attitude toward Guy. Suddenly, it dawned on me. The reason we struggled so much was because I didn't have a "Me First Attitude" in our marriage. And neither did Guy. I know. It may sound surprising and unbiblical, this advocacy for having a "Me First Attitude." The Bible teaches us *not* to think of ourselves first, but stay with me. Read the following verses with your attitude toward your spouse in mind:

Romans 12:10 (ESV): "Love one another with brotherly affection. Outdo one another in showing honor."

Do you wake up in the morning seeking ways you can "outdo" your wife or husband in showing her/him honor? Is brotherly or marital affection a trademark of your relationship? If not, this passage would serve you well to meditate and pray on as part of your daily habits.

Galatians 5:13 (ESV): "For you were called to freedom, brothers. Only do not use your freedom as an opportunity for the flesh, but through love serve one another."

Just because we *can* do something doesn't mean we *should*. If there is any attitude that you feel justified in, but it is harming your relationship, you are not free to have that attitude. Imagine if both husband and wife used the freedom of their relationship to serve through love. What if we really believed that it is better to give than to receive? Ask yourself honestly, is your desire to serve your wife/husband more important to you than getting your own way?

John 13:34 (ESV): "A new commandment I give to you, that you love one another: just as I have loved you, you also are to love one another."

Let's think about this verse. Jesus isn't giving us any caveats here. No conditions apply. Consider what it cost Jesus to love well, and then go and do the same.

Proverbs 11:25 (ESV): "Whoever brings blessing will be enriched, and one who waters will himself be watered."

Does it feel like having a "Me First Attitude" might be the death of you? It should. It should very much be the death of "self." The beautiful paradox is that by "watering" and blessing our husbands and wives, we are the ones who are "watered." The more we pour out, the more we are filled. This thinking defies logic, but that's what faith always

If there is any attitude that you feel justified in, but it is harming your relationship, you are not free to have that attitude.

does. Is your attitude one that seeks to refresh your spouse? Do you want to have a strong and healthy marriage? The grass isn't greener on the other side. Justin Bieber is right. It's green where you water it.

As these verses spoke to my heart, I pray they are speaking to yours. I wasn't going to have a more peaceful and happy home when Guy changed his attitude. I was going to *be* more peaceful and happier by having the same attitude as Jesus Christ toward Guy. When we were lost, Jesus was first to seek us and find us. When we were sinful, Jesus was first to grace us. When we were selfish, Jesus was first to serve us. When we were unlovely, Jesus was first to love us. This is what having a "Me First Attitude" is all about. Being Me First–minded is exactly what we must do for true biblical love to bloom in our marriages. It's the only attitude adjustment we need for our marriages to blossom into what God designed them to be.

When a disagreement happens, *be first*. Be the first to sincerely apologize, taking ownership of your wrongdoing.

When you hurt each other's feelings, *be first*. Be the first to go to your wife/husband and offer empathy for how she/he feels.

When your expectations are unmet, *be first*. Be the first to spend time with God rearranging those expectations and then do the work to clearly communicate.

When you want your husband to be the example of leading your family in prayer, *be first*. Pray with your family without feeling resentful that it was your idea.

When you both have had a long and grueling day, *be first*. Be the one to keep going a little bit longer at your own expense so that your spouse can unwind.

When you want your husband to plan a romantic date, *be*

first. Make a plan with him in mind from a loving and generous heart.

When you asked him to do a certain task around the house and it's still not done, *be first.* Surprise yourself with your knack and ability to attempt it on your own. Do so with a spirit of loving service.

When the dishes are still piled in the sink, *be first.* Be first to jump in and relieve the burden of housework.

What would you add to this list? This is not a selfish me-first attitude. It's about being "me first" in order to make things right, to lovingly and sincerely serve your family, and to honor God by doing so. A loving marriage is established by loving attitudes. Loving attitudes are established by loving thoughts. Loving thoughts are established by loving actions. Loving actions are established by obeying God's Word.

One warning here for the couple who has been entrenched in negativity and whose angry reactions are the norm. When one person begins to transform by the Word of God, it may not be immediately well received by the other spouse. Our godly character doesn't always comfort them. It *convicts* them. Some of us respond to conviction by allowing it to catapult us toward change. Others become aware of the sharp contrast in attitudes and instead of allowing that conviction to do its good work, they allow their pride to rule their hearts, becoming even more resistant to gentle biblical

> *A loving marriage is established by loving attitudes. Loving attitudes are established by loving thoughts. Loving thoughts are established by loving actions. Loving actions are established by obeying God's Word.*

responses. I remember a roommate with whom I had this experience. The kinder I treated her, the nastier she became. The more Christ-like my words and responses to triggers, the more mean-spirited her reactions. If this happens in your marriage, don't lose heart. Remember that Jesus was treated much the same, and count yourself blessed to be able to identify with Christ in His sufferings. Never give up praying for your spouse, and the overwhelming testimony of your godly character will win him/her over. Take comfort from this description in The Message of 1 Peter 3:13–16 (MSG):

"If with heart and soul you're doing good, do you think you can be stopped? Even if you suffer for it, you're still better off . . . Keep a clear conscience before God so that when people throw mud at you, none of it will stick. They'll end up realizing that *they're* the ones who need a bath."

Guy and I eventually finished that picture wall in our first home together. Instead of nailing happy family portraits into the walls, our attitudes could have been the nails in our coffins. It serves as a reminder that even when our attitudes aren't always a mirror image of Christ, we can still come together, adjusting our mind-sets for the good of one another. Resentment can so easily take up residence in our homes, an invisible picture of discontent that has no rightful place on anyone's wall of memories, but if our hearts are Christ's home, then we can usher bitterness on out the door by the power of the Holy Spirit.

Triggers in our marriages are opportunities for us to make attitude adjustments, letting go of bitterness and pain. The moment you begin to feel the heat rise, feel the first twinge of guilt, or see the wave of conflict begin to overtake you, remember that you can be first. That's Jesus' example to us. Romans 5:8 (NASB) says, "But God demonstrates his own love for us, in that while we were yet sinners, Christ died for us." Your husband is still a sinner. Your wife is still a sinner. Regardless, we have the privilege to put on a godly attitude. It's the ultimate example of love and the foundation for a picture-perfect marriage.

Let's Pray: "Lord Jesus, you are the ultimate example of having a 'Me First Attitude.' You did not think of Yourself when you humbly entered this world as a vulnerable baby. Your desire to love and save me is what led You to give Your very life for my sake. How could I not also be willing to have a 'Me First Attitude' in every aspect of my marriage? Remove the fear that I will be taken advantage of. Help me to love my wife/husband with the love You have loved me with as an act of worship to You. Lord, I ask this same attitude to be my wife's/husband's attitude. Let us be filled to overflowing because we continually bless and 'water' one another. Let Your Word wash over us and transform us. In Jesus' Name, Amen!"

CHAPTER 23

WHEN YOU NEED A VISION
FOR YOUR MARRIAGE (GUY)

When Amber and I first started dating, we began a tradition of having our friends over on January 1 for an evening of fellowship and prayer. We cut out pictures and words from magazines that represented our hopes, dreams, and goals. As we pasted them onto poster boards, they became a tangible image of the things we envisioned for the year ahead and the desires of our hearts. Each item represented became a prayer point as we yielded them to God and entrusted our desires to His will for our lives.

Over the years, Amber and I have led small groups through our church and mentored men and women on their spiritual paths. Many problems couples faced in their marriages resulted from a lack of intention in their relationships. When a couple feels aimless, they can feel stuck or restless, which can give way to moodiness, frustration, and irritability. As God's children, we are all designed with purpose, so if our marriages lack vision, that void becomes a trigger. Discontent seeps in and before we know it, we are unhappy in our marriages, but we can't put our finger on why. Some of our biggest marriage triggers don't result from what we do but from what we neglect to do. If we haven't carefully considered what God's purpose is for our specific union as a couple, and if we aren't working together toward fulfilling all that God has for us, our relationship can feel like a scratchy wool sweater instead of a perfectly fitted glove.

While digging around in the garage recently, Amber and I found two of the first vision boards we made during our engagement. Ironically, we had a lot of similar dreams and goals, though they reflected different tones—Amber's board was bright and beachy, covered with pictures of island scenes and interior designs of living rooms and kitchens. Healthy food, Nike

> *Some of our biggest marriage triggers don't result from what we do but from what we neglect to do.*

running shoes, and Bible verses scattered across her board. Mine was darker and more focused on nature, with images of mountains, couples wearing hiking boots, rugged tents, Jeeps, and hang gliders.

Going into our first year of marriage, we anticipated enjoying the world around us, setting up our new home together, and trusting God for our new future as a couple. We had no idea that our first year of marriage would include a difficult pregnancy, troubled relationships with extended family, and new financial pressures. As years went by, we learned to hold our dreams loosely, but having a visual of the longings in our hearts planted seeds of much needed optimism and faith in God to help us accomplish the good works He created us to do—especially when our circumstances threw us a curveball.

Having a vision for what God can do in our lives prevents us from feeling like spectators in our own lives. Michael Hyatt, a motivational speaker, entrepreneur, and Christian author, advocates the idea of a Life Plan that we can easily adopt in our marriages. He says:

"Sadly, I have met very few people who have a plan for their life. Most are passive spectators, watching their lives unfold, one day at a time. They are reactive rather than proactive. They may plan their careers, the building of a new home, or even a vacation. But it never occurs to them to plan their life. In fact, most people spend more time planning a one-week vacation than they spend planning their life. I believe that this is why so many people end up discouraged, disillusioned, and wondering what went wrong. They arrived at the wrong destination."[24]

Marriage is no different. In fact, the stakes are much higher, especially when you add children into the mix. The lack of a life plan for your marriage can easily cause two separate journeys on two different paths that never find their intersection. The intersection of two life paths is where a great marriage begins. It is also where a family finds its combined purpose. When you and your spouse are wandering through life on separate paths, having different experiences, you exist in a place filled with misunderstanding, misaligned goals, and a lack of direction. With so many misses, the situation becomes a highly triggered environment.

Luckily, because of the work Amber and I did early in our relationship, many of our goals for our family were aligned. We agreed about how many kids we wanted to have on our first date! Three seemed like a good number for both of us, but God gave us a happy bonus with our fourth son three years ago. Still, having an idea about what our family would look like enabled us to support one another and become a team.

Several years ago, Amber and I took an evening and wrote out a handful of dreams and goals we wanted to accomplish in one-year, five-year, and ten-year increments. We categorized them as personal goals, career goals, and family goals, including things like running a 5K race, publishing a book, and homeschooling our kids for a year in order to travel. We also wrote down adoption, producing TV shows and films that honor God and inspire others, and taking a mission's trip with our kids.

After making our lists separately, we came together to compare and then blend them. Then we sat down with our calendars and penciled in specific dates and action steps so we would follow through. While we understand that God's will for us may look a bit different, we have found that having these goals written down and prayed over regularly keeps us on track and brings a sense of unity and purpose to our relationship. *The intersection of two life paths is where a great marriage begins.* We are able to prioritize how we spend our time and what commitments we make. It helps us say "no" more easily to the things that will only clog the process of achievements and work we want to do for the Lord. We also got a glimpse of the issues that matter to each of us, which drew our hearts together. That has been invaluable in helping us make decisions for ourselves and our family and take faith risks that have resulted in significant spiritual growth.

An acquaintance of mine recently shared that he and his wife were not on the same wavelength, which was causing stress and arguments on a regular basis. They have young children who are thriving in public school and busy with athletics, theater, etc. Because he works as an independent contractor, which can be precarious and sporadic, his wife reentered the workforce to provide some stability for their family. Her full-time job suddenly became a much bigger commitment after she got a promotion and new responsibilities. She did not want to be working outside of the home, but she felt they "needed" the security of her career. While her job offered the best health care and consistent paychecks, his was a pursuit of passion and what he felt "called" to do. Unfortunately, due to their schedules and the craziness of life, he and his wife had not had collective conversations about goals, schedules, and mutual passions. As a result, they fell into an unhealthy pattern of coexisting, simply sharing responsibilities involving the kids, and in many ways, leading separate lives. Their lack of unity of heart left a dangerous opportunity for Satan to plant seeds of discontent, distance, and bitterness in their marriage.

Whether you create a vision board, map out a life plan, or develop your own method for creating a vision for your marriage and family, the important foundation is that this concept directly aligns with your faith. God is without a doubt a planner. He makes it clear that He has a vision for each one of us. In fact, He had a vision for you long before you were even born! Psalm 139:13 (NIV) says, "For you created my inmost being; you knit me together in my mother's womb." He did this so you, and eventually you and your spouse together, would fulfill His good plans for your life.

Jeremiah 29:11 (NIV) further expands on this biblical concept: "'For I know the plans I have for you,' declares the Lord, 'plans to prosper you and not to harm you, plans to give you hope and a future.'"

God's words to Jeremiah reveal His heart. His character is one that longs to bless His children with good things to look forward to. That's you and me—and you and your spouse!

Marriage is at its core a sacrificial engagement. It is not a singular fulfillment of your own personal goals alone, but the fulfillment of God's plan for you both. The very fact that God brought you together in a marriage union is an assurance that He also expects you to be unified in your vision together. The two of you are more effective for the Kingdom as a couple than if you had remained single. Ultimately, God's purpose for our marriages is not for our own carnal fulfillment but for His glory. Keeping that in mind helps us to be selfless as we work toward supporting the hopes and dreams of our spouse.

The Message translation of Proverbs 29:18 says, "If people can't see what God is doing, they stumble all over themselves; But when they attend to what he reveals, they are most blessed."

Does your marriage feel aimless? Stagnant? Does this lead to arguments and tension in your marriage? Do you feel like you are stumbling over yourselves? The benefit of having a vision for your relationship isn't simply about self-fulfillment; it allows us to see God's hand in our lives, increasing our faith and giving us joy!

In Robert Frost's poem "The Road Not Taken," he writes that "two roads diverged in a yellow wood." The narrator of the poem must decide whether to take the predictable, easier-looking path or the less predictable one, "the one less traveled by." It's all well and good to wrestle with which path to take in life when it's your own decision to make and live with, but when you have a spouse and a family, those choices become more complicated and the stakes become exponentially higher. When husbands and wives lack direction or vision, marriage can feel aimless and, worse yet, pointless. But God made us for a purpose, and He designed our homes to be purpose-filled too. Working together to create a vision for our marriages aligns us with God's will, and there's no better place for a couple to be.

Let's Pray: "Dear Lord God, thank You for Your reassurances that long before I was born You had a plan for my life, and our family. Sometimes life can be so challenging that I lose focus and direction. I pray, Lord, that You would make our goals clear and align our hearts together in new ways. We don't want to drift through life. Help us make the most of every opportunity so that we can fulfill the good works You have created us to do! We trust You, Lord, to do with our desires what You will. Help us to trust You if the path we take seems challenging or our dreams take longer to come to fruition than we would like. Make us a team, unified in every way. In Jesus' Name, Amen!"

CHAPTER 24

WHEN YOUR PERSONALITIES CLASH (AMBER)

I pulled into the church parking lot and hurried into the already crowded auditorium. Dr. Neil Clark Warren, relationship expert and founder of the Christian dating website eHarmony, was about to take the stage. As a clinical psychologist and theologian, Dr. Warren has researched and written extensively about the complex challenge of finding, attracting, and selecting the right marriage partner. Eager to find my own life partner, I wasn't about to miss one word.

Throughout his message, Dr. Warren suggested marrying someone who is as similar to you as possible, alleviating many triggers toward frustration and anger. His own parents struggled to communicate, as they had vast differences in their intelligence and interests. Witnessing this in his home at a young age, Dr. Warren saw that compatibility is a key factor in harmony between couples. As I listened, the old saying "Opposites attract" didn't sound so appealing in the long run.

Several years later, I sat on my living room floor as a newlywed, rifling through stacks of old sermon and lecture notes from over the years. I stumbled upon the notes I took during Warren's message that lonely evening. His words jumped off the pages, and my heart sank. I had not taken his message seriously and ended up marrying a man who was very much my opposite— one of Warren's strongest cautions when choosing a husband or wife. Guy's personality and mine were less compatible than I realized, and it was taking a toll.

Before we continue, take a moment to write down three main personality differences between you and your wife or husband that often leave you triggered. Now, how can each of those be a positive instead of a negative? Are you open to viewing your spouse's differences as strengths more often than weaknesses?

A planner myself, Guy's spontaneous, laid-back personality often made me feel like I was carrying the weight of orchestrating our daily lives. That pressure irritated me, and I felt quick to judge. My tendency to micromanage Guy felt suffocating to him, and my very passionate personality often came across as too aggressive for his more casual approach to conversations. His sensitive spirit often felt wounded by our interactions, leaving me guessing how I could possibly please him when he was so easily offended. Can you relate to any of that?

The good news is that Guy and I are more alike now than ever. We chose to have open minds, viewing one another as assets, not liabilities. It's a trigger we still continue to work on, practicing believing the best about one another instead of getting quick to anger. Guy keeps us grounded as the realist, helping us avoid risky pitfalls, whereas I help us shoot for the stars as the optimist and visionary. As mutual extroverts, we rarely have arguments over hosting parties, attending work events, or escaping on adventures together.

The glue that holds us together, despite our personality differences, is the overarching values we agree on: our commitment to the Lord, our willingness to parent on the same page, and our dreams for our family's future as a whole. These core values continue to serve as a compass for walking on the same path together, eventually reaching our goals, and allowing me to be more open to Guy's way of getting there, and vice versa. We may rabbit-trail along, but we eventually reach our destination.

Your spouse's personality differences create your unique marriage personality. Sometimes you must be willing to go off the beaten path—by embracing your spouse's way of doing things—trusting that you will reach the desired destination in the end. For Guy and me, that means I need to ease up on my tendency to plan every detail of every moment, and Guy gets to grow in appreciation for my businesslike tone.

He learns to take more risks, and I learn to let our boys be spontaneous. Instead of viewing my way of doing things as the best way, I get to grow in humility, embracing and

> *Your spouse's personality differences create your unique marriage personality.*

appreciating my husband's uniqueness. Learning to truly value your differences can make or break you. Your spouse's personality was not meant to trigger you, it was designed to complement you. Guy says, "If we were both the same, we wouldn't be able to catch each other when we are down, because we'd both be down." He's so right! We get to cherish and support one another best, because we are different.

Proverbs 11:2 (NLT) says, "Pride leads to disgrace, but with humility comes wisdom." There are few things more disgraceful than ugly, angry reactions when our spouses don't com-

Your spouse's personality was not meant to trigger you, it was designed to complement you.

municate or do things the way we do. Assuming that their personality is inferior to ours is prideful. I don't know about you, but I need all the wisdom I can get. God tells us clearly that we will grow in wisdom when we grow in humility. If your personality differences cause lots of frustration in your marriage, are you willing to think more positively about the traits that distinguish you from one another? What can you overlook? How can you affirm the differences that typically you undervalue? What's one thing you can say to be a peacemaker when you feel triggered?

Recently, I took a poll asking married couples if their personalities were opposite from one another. Hundreds of families responded. Seventy-five percent said that their personalities were very different from their spouse's personality. Many agreed that it can cause problem after problem, but most couples expressed that over time, they grew to appreciate their differences.

One reader echoed what so many others had to say about the personality differences in their marriages. Sarah wrote:

"I'd say we were opposites in personality when we married and yet shared similar values and many years as friends, which gave us much in common. As we've now been married 21 years, we've grown to be more alike, and yet several differences continue to keep us growing together! We were told before we married that the things that we loved most about one another would eventually be the things that got on our nerves most . . . so true. He is spontaneous, which balances my desire for order and control. He is an introvert, while I'm more of a people person. He is logical, while my emotions often run wild. He loves to get dirty and rough it, while I prefer the cleaner, gentler things in life, but I'm so thankful for all these checks and balances."

Emily, another reader, put it this way: "It really depends on the day and my heart posture. Sometimes if I'm not looking at him as a gift from God and I'm being critical, the differences seem like a big deal. On the other hand, if my heart posture is in the right place, then those differences seem like a gift and a complement to my own personality."

Love looks a lot like accepting one another unconditionally, just as God does. When we were at our worst, He looked on us with compassion and love. Take a look at 1 John 4:7 (NIV): "Dear friends, let us love one another, for love comes from God. Everyone who loves has been born of God and knows God."

If we claim to be Christ-followers, celebrating our differences should be a priority. It's an opportunity to demonstrate the love of God to our husbands and wives. Marriage is meant to be a place where love grows. If spouses do not feel valued for who they are, deep in their core, then it's pretty hard for them to feel loved. Angry reactions over personality differences rob us of our potential to learn, grow, and thrive.

The truth of the matter is that our spouses' personalities probably are not going to change drastically. And yet, we can have a drastic impact on the quality of our relationship when we put on the humility of Jesus Christ, seeking to appreciate and embrace our differences. God

> *Marriage is meant to be a place where love grows. If spouses do not feel valued for who they are, deep in their core, then it's pretty hard to feel loved.*

didn't make a mistake when He molded you in your mother's womb, nor did He make a mistake when he fashioned your husband or wife. In His Sovereignty, He brought you together, to be a blessing one to another.

Let's Pray: "Father, You did a good work in bringing me and my spouse together. You made him/her just the way You wanted to. And You designed me with a specific purpose too. I desire to appreciate our differences, but sometimes it's so hard. We clash instead of complement one another. I want us to grow in humility and love! Lord, please aid us in this. Open my eyes and my heart to appreciate him/her more. Help me to see the value in our personality differences. Let us think of each other more than ourselves. Jesus, I trust that You will help us to find mutual appreciation for our unique personalities. In Jesus' Name, Amen!"

CHAPTER 25

WHEN YOU NEED TO KNOW THAT GOD SEES YOU IN YOUR TRIGGERED MARRIAGE (AMBER)

$\mathcal{S}$ ometimes, the biggest trigger in our lives is when we wonder if God cares about our daily struggles. Our triggered reactions may have little to do with our spouse and everything to do with a crisis of our own faith. We wonder if God sees us and if the tensions between us matter to Him. Our minds spin with questions for God. Where is He when our wife turns cold or our husband works too much? Can He heal our loneliness or change our spouse's mind? How long must we keep persevering when so many problems in our relationship abound? We lose sleep at night wondering if He will help us in our time of need, and the crisis of our faith strains our relationship further.

Most of the time, we are called to walk by faith through our troubles. Hebrews 11:1 (NIV) says, "Now faith is confidence in what we hope for and assurance about what we do not see." God doesn't always reveal Himself in grandiose ways; rather, He prompts us to walk by faith, not by sight. The act of trusting Him when we can't see or feel Him is part of our faith journey. Pastor

Rick Warren, author of the best-selling book *The Purpose Driven Life*, puts it this way:

> "God is real, no matter how you feel. It is easy to worship God when things are going great in your life—when he has provided food, friends, family, health, and happy situations. But circumstances are not always pleasant. How do you worship God then? What do you do when God seems a million miles away?
>
> "The deepest level of worship is praising God in spite of pain, thanking God during a trial, trusting him when tempted, surrendering while suffering, and loving him when he seems distant."[25]

Does God feel distant? One of the best ways we can find peace in the midst of our marriage problems is to remember His faithfulness to us in the past and to be inspired by the testimonies of God's power in the lives of others. I believe God allowed the story I'm about to share with you to serve as a "memorial" for me of His presence in my life and His ability to solve any of my problems. God knew that when my anger toward my husband reached a breaking point, I would need assurance that He brought us together as man and wife.

You see, God may seem distant, but He is not. God knows what we need. He proved this to me repeatedly over one devastating month when I needed Him to show up. It was at a time when the circumstances of my life were ideal, and then instantly, everything changed.

I was dating a man I wanted to marry, feeling fulfilled as a high school English teacher, and dreaming about the happy future I was entering. Suddenly, I was unexpectedly single again, blindsided, heartbroken, and shattered. Realizing that my hopes for marriage were now altering my life's choices, I felt directionless. I loved teaching, but the low pay was a sacrifice, and my true passion was to be a stay-at-home mom. I longed to travel the world, enjoy recreational activities, and someday buy my own home. Those dreams vaporized. I knew I could not do some of those things on my own and I was tired of being alone. The world was bleak, indeed.

I spent my days waking with tears and going to bed with tears. It was the middle of February. I had a mega-heartache, an empty bank account and financial debt, and no direction for my career.

Within two weeks of the breakup, I somehow managed to get a sold-out spot to join two hundred Christian singles at a retreat in Mammoth for a ski weekend. It was an attempt on my part to change the scenery and find a small distraction from my grief. My girlfriend and I had a great time skiing that first day, and later we soaked in massive twenty-person hot tubs with other church friends to ease our muscles. We met new people that night and started lifelong friendships. The next day was spent on the slopes before making the trip back to reality. It was just what I needed.

Still battling intense sadness, I started attending a small study group with some friends as we read through Rick Warren's *The Purpose Driven Life.* One night, a girl in our study group shared that she had been praying for God to take away her financial debt. I thought to myself, "I have never prayed for that!" I had been slowly chipping away at my debt and had several thousand dollars still to go. On a private school teacher's salary, it was daunting. That night, I prayed a simple prayer: "Lord, remove my debt!"

During my quiet time of Bible study and prayer, I had also been praying that God would reveal Himself to me as His cherished daughter, He my Heavenly Father—I needed His comfort so desperately. The next day, I woke early and spent time grieving with the Lord, longing for Him to comfort me as a father comforts a daughter, to give me a vision for my future, and to provide.

The workday went smoothly and when I got home that afternoon, I scooped up the mail. As I readied myself to go to the gym for a workout, I quickly scanned the envelopes. One of them was a statement for my credit card, so I tore it open. It confused me entirely. The balance was $0.00. I had not paid it off, and I still owed a significant amount. Thinking there was a mistake, I called the company. The operator confirmed that I had a zero-dollar balance and that I actually had a credit of $300, which she would send to me in the form of a check. I feebly thanked her and hung up the phone. Bewildered, I decided to go to the gym and sort out the mess later. After my workout, as I was driving home, I remembered that I had prayed the night before that God would take away my debt. I raced up the stairs and looked at the date of the statement. It was for the month prior. God had erased my debt, and He had answered my prayer a month before I prayed it. I dropped to my knees. Frantically, I called my dad, who was on a business trip. He answered the phone. I excitedly poured out that I had prayed about my debt, and suddenly, my debt was gone. I figured it was a mistake and I feared a huge hassle and mess, but just maybe God had answered my prayer. "Amber, Amber," my father delightedly said, interrupting me. "I paid your debt." "What?" I stammered. I knew he was not able to do such a thing, and yet he did! I was overwhelmed with thankfulness and cried tears of happiness. My Heavenly Father had answered *two* of my prayers. He wiped out my debt, and He used my earthly father to demonstrate His love for me as my Heavenly Father, I his cherished daughter.

Later that same week, I went to church, where my pastor, Francis Chan, was teaching in Revelation. It was a powerful teaching series that laid out the utter and total holiness of God. As Francis taught that Sunday, he made the truth of seeing the holiness of the Lord filling the temple and the awe-inspiring awesomeness of His character come alive. He shared that he had had to lie down with his face to the ground in worship as he prepared and studied for the message because he was so overcome by God's mighty power. *It stuck with me.*

The days continued. Still feeling lost, unloved, and alone, I was questioning everything about my future, including my career as a teacher. Knowing I was back to being single and providing for myself, I prayed that this Holy God would give me direction in my job. As summer approached, I realized that I was going to have a lot of free time on my hands, but with no one to spend it with, or the funds to travel or do the things that I would love to do. I prayed that this Mighty God would give me something, *anything*, to look forward to.

The next workday came, and I received an email from a committee that I had applied to the year before about the possibility of furthering my education. I clicked the open button. The letter told me that I was accepted into a program with a full grant, worth tens of thousands of dollars, to earn my master's degree from Grand Canyon University in Arizona. My jaw literally dropped. I had applied but hadn't believed I would actually get the chance to pursue graduate school. The letter told me that I would begin classes in the next month. It would be an accelerated two-year program with no more than twenty-four hours off between classes, but in the end, I would have a master's degree in Leadership and Educational Administration—the next step up for me in my career. I began to shake. "Lord, how can You be so good?" I prayed, overwhelmed. I sat at my desk and cried, "Too much, Lord, too much!" God had answered my prayer for direction for my future and my career and also provided the funds to do it.

Only a day or two later, I arrived for work and took my seat for the usual 7:15 A.M. staff meeting. Afterward, one of my colleagues approached me. He explained that through unforeseen circumstances, two of the chaperones that he had lined up to take with him on a mission's trip to Argentina for the next two summers had to back out. There was a paid ticket waiting for the right person to join them on a scouting trip in just a few months' time and then to take a follow-up trip with students the next year. He asked me to pray about the possibility of taking the trip with them as a chaperone.

I couldn't believe my ears! The Lord knew I wanted to travel, and I had petulantly been complaining in my prayers that I had no chance of that in my budget. He had heard me and answered my prayer for something that was not a necessity, but a pleasure.

I walked in a daze to my classroom; the surreal nature of the last two weeks was beyond my imagination. A few days later, I let my colleague know that I was honored to go with him and to serve in Argentina. However, the worrier in me began to fret to God about affording the several hundred dollars I would need for spending money on the trip. But just a few days later, I got an enigmatic email from the administration office asking me to stop by during my break.

I was a little nervous as I made way down to the office. The secretary took me in the back to a safe and opened it up. She handed me a plain white envelope and said that someone "anonymously wanted me to have this." I thanked her and hurried back to my empty classroom. I sat in my chair, the envelope unopened on my desk before me. Fingers trembling, I opened it up and out fell several hundred dollars. God had answered my prayer for spending money on the trip to Argentina. "Overwhelmed" doesn't sufficiently describe the way I felt. My heart was so full of gratitude to God! He had revealed that He was there, listening, seeing me in all of my loss, and providing for my heart's desires. I, too, like my pastor had taught that Sunday, saw the holiness of God, mighty to save, seeing me, hearing me, loving me. I, too, fell facedown on the floor, there on the ground in the middle of my classroom, and wept.

But the story doesn't end there.

I went on that trip to Argentina, traveling for several weeks with four dear colleagues, laughing, serving God, and trying to heal. One day, we visited the romantic Iguazu Falls on the border of Argentina and Brazil. The magnificence of the falls takes your breath away. At one point, I found myself standing alone in "Lover's Cove," and as I looked over the waters, I wanted to weep from the loneliness that overwhelmed me in my singleness. It was a wonderful trip, but also difficult at times as I continued to struggle with my grief.

The next year I focused on my graduate work, choosing not to date, praying for God to provide a husband for me in His time. The healing came. After a

> *He had revealed that He was there, listening, seeing me in all of my loss, and providing for my heart's desires.*

year had gone by, I opened my heart up to begin dating a friend I knew from church. A few short months later, I was preparing to leave for my next trip with students to Argentina. When my boyfriend learned that we were one male chaperone short, he eagerly volunteered. His offer was readily accepted by my school. Part of our trip was to revisit Iguazu Falls. As we entered Lover's Cove, my boyfriend, Guy Lia, got down on one knee and asked me to marry him. The amazing thing about this? I had met him for the very first time on that ski trip a year earlier, after my breakup, in the same month that God had answered all my other deeply passionate prayers! The first order of business that God took into consideration when my broken heart pleaded with Him for the pain to ease was to introduce me unknowingly to my future husband. He then blessed me by restoring my hope with a proposal in that special place where I had stood a year before, once broken, now restored.

There are times when we pray and God will seem distant. He doesn't always answer our prayers with an immediate "yes." Sometimes, He says "no" or asks us to wait. But at a time when I knew I was being faithful and chose to trust Him in my brokenness, He stood before me in the form of my circumstances and showed me that He alone is the One who can repair my heart, grant me my most private and personal desires, and bless me beyond measure. Lest you think that God is not real, that He is not present in your everyday lives, able to intervene in your marriage, stop and consider how gracious He was to me and honestly ask Him to reveal Himself to you. Decide for yourself that you will trust Him, and that you will praise Him even when He is silent, and you just might discover that He is near you, orchestrating your life in beautiful ways.

Can God handle our daily struggles in our marriages? Yes, He can. Does He sometimes feel distant or uncaring? At times. Relying on our feelings or circumstances as evidence for God's desire to help us is always a mistake. He sees You. He is able. As part of the Church, you are Christ's beloved, joined in spiritual marriage. How could He forget you? How could your earthly marriage escape His care? Prayerfully seek Him, releasing your anger and frustrations to Him. And sometimes . . . sometimes, when you really need it, He may just do for you what is beyond your ability to ask or imagine.

> *As part of the Church, you are Christ's beloved, joined in spiritual marriage. How could He forget you? How could your earthly marriage escape His care?*

Let's Pray: "Heavenly Father, you are good. You see me. You know me. My marriage problems are not a surprise to You. Lord, you have felt distant at times and the pain of feeling alone and lost in my marriage can overwhelm me. I never want to think that You are not with me in my marriage. That You don't see me. Lord, thank You for increasing my faith and giving me the assurance of what I cannot see. I trust You that You will carry me and my husband/wife through as we face our marriage triggers. I believe that You can and will do exceedingly abundantly, beyond all we could ask or imagine. We are filled with hope as we wait on You to reveal Your presence in our lives and in our relationship. In Jesus' Name, Amen!"

CHAPTER 26

WHEN YOUR UPBRINGINGS WERE DIFFERENT (AMBER)

*P*astor Chuck Swindoll says, "We cannot change our past. We cannot change the fact that people act in a certain way. We cannot change the inevitable. The only thing we can do is play on the one string we have, and that is our attitude."[26]

The ways we are raised impact our lives deeply, both in personality and behavior development as well as the customs and traditions we hold. Carefully consider the following questions: What two words come to mind that describe your childhood? What words would your spouse use to describe his or hers? What are some of your family traditions and customs? And your spouse's? It's easy to become triggered when we go into marriage assuming that our spouse will simply drop into our life as we know it. Whether you had an ideal upbringing or are determined to do things differently, the place where many of us go wrong is assuming our way is the best or only way. Same old scene, new actors. It doesn't work like that, however. This mentality sets us up for conflict.

Married life draws two unique people together to make a

new one-of-a-kind-life. It's not meant to duplicate one or the other's own upbringing and when couples seek to follow traditions that clash, knee-jerk reactions often result. One spouse may dig in his heels while the other feels bulldozed. We go into marriage feeling united by our love until we are triggered by the need to do things as we have always done them and are met with resistance.

When I consider the words that describe my own childhood, "volatile yet happy" come to mind. My father was a brilliant businessman in the field of aerospace and also a jewelry designer, my mother a talented cook and stay-at-home-mom. My older brother and I are third-generation Californians, and all of us, naturally, are beach bums. Having been raised in the aftermath of my parents' excommunication from a strict separatist religious cult, there was little rhyme or reason to many of our family practices. The process of deprogramming and the anger and depression that went with it is not the ideal stuff of child-rearing. I never knew what a day might bring. Yet, my parents went out of their way to give us a wonderful life—full of generosity and love as best they could give it. They taught us the Bible and helped us memorize verses. We traveled, raised a veritable zoo of pets, and attended high-achieving private schools.

Guy describes his childhood as wonderful and challenging. He was born to older parents, who doted on him and his siblings. Family was everything and Guy has fond memories of adventurous weekend road trips, family musical theater, and earning his Eagle Scout badge. When he was a young boy, both of his parents—an electrician for the military and a registered nurse—retired, making themselves available in ways many parents can't. Regulars at church, they served others, gladly. Sadly, they both suffered the residuals of injuries from car accidents and other serious health issues that created financial woes. Far too early, Guy would lose his dad to a sudden heart attack, while his mother survived several massive strokes and was wheelchair-bound by the time Guy was in his early twenties, leaving him to navigate his life without their wisdom and support.

My upbringing shaped me into someone who has a strong need for justice and for nurture. It also made me needy. I craved kindness in the everyday moments of life—and those needs fueled some of the biggest triggers with Guy once we were married. If I perceived anything he said or did as remotely unkind, I panicked. It brought up unsavory memories from my childhood. I felt like the person who was supposed to love me best didn't really love me at all. And I reacted. The problem is you can't demand love—or the way you need to feel loved—from another person. My strong need for justice made arguing with me much like standing before a prosecutor on the witness stand instead of a loving wife.

Guy's childhood shaped him into a deeply sensitive person. He developed a thirst for adventure, but he often felt directionless and unmotivated. His lack of personal drive made me feel insecure, and that fueled my neediness. Growing up, Guy was doted on quite a bit, the star of his family and well liked at school. When the cold, hard world hit, he didn't have the life skills to overcome the hardships. It was a difficult road learning to persevere in the face of opposition as an adult, especially without parents to guide him. His sensitive spirit made it impossible for me to do anything right. I could offer what I deemed constructive criticism and Guy would take it personally. I needed him to toughen up, and yet I didn't want him to lose the emotional side that also made our relationship so special. Had we given in to our triggers, I'm certain we would have become a divorce statistic.

Many of our personality differences fall into the great nature-versus-nurture debate, though I think we can all agree that our upbringings influenced our natural temperaments.

The way our parents raised us also had different spiritual undertones, views about money, and holiday traditions. I'm betting you understand exactly what I'm talking about. Often, couples don't realize the impact and influence of their family dynamics on their marriage until they begin fighting over how to spend summer vacation, whose house to visit for Christmas, which spouse will be in charge of paying bills, or what time dinner should be served. These triggers are rooted in our childhoods. The beauty of traditions and customs loses its luster when they become trigger points. I believe we could avoid many of our marriage triggers if we didn't attach so much importance to our ideals and instead put more importance on our spouse's feelings. If you value your customs so much that it causes anger in your marriage, you are valuing the wrong thing. No tradition or family practice is more significant than your significant other. It's perfectly normal and healthy to take some of the best of your childhood practices and tweak them to be your own as a couple or abandon them completely for something new. God values making things new. The apostle Paul writes:

"So then, if anyone is in Christ, he is a new creation; what is old has passed away—look, what is new has come!" (2 Corinthians 5:17, NET)

"Put on your new nature, and be renewed as you learn to know your Creator and become like him . . . Christ is all that matters, and he lives in all of us." (Colossians 3:10–11, NLT)

The church at that time was learning to navigate religious and cultural traditions in light of their newfound Christianity. Paul encouraged his followers to see themselves through the eyes of Jesus, not through old habits or mind-sets. The only thing that mattered personally and collectively was Christ—and that Jesus lived inside of them. The same is true for us when we think about marriage. The tone of our homes should be consistent with people whose hearts are Christ's home.

If you value your customs so much that it causes anger in your marriage, you are valuing the wrong thing. No tradition or family practice is more significant than your significant other.

Knowing that Guy didn't have much accountability growing up helps me to be compassionate when he struggles to follow through on a project around the house. Because Guy knows that I missed out on a lot of celebratory traditions, he is open-minded about the manic pace I set around birthdays and special events. He is patient with me, joining in with gusto instead of making me feel guilty for spending money or dismissing what matters to me.

What would happen if you showed your in-laws mercy by inviting them into your home for special occasions? How might your spouse's love for you grow if you humbly apologized more often? What could happen if you stopped trying to change that quirky thing your spouse does that usually drives you crazy? We are new creations in Christ. We are new people when we get married. We can relate to our spouses with the heart of Jesus when we see that they are still a work in progress, because we are too. Anger sucks away our energy. Our energy should be spent making the most of our opportunities as a new couple, not warring over them. Socrates said, "The secret of change is to focus all of your energy, not on fighting the old, but on building the new."[27] I think he's onto something there.

Honestly, the Christian life is not easy. It involves sacrifice, and yet the selflessness we may display pales in comparison to the selflessness of the Lord Jesus. His example to us dissipates our need to fulfill our own desires and extinguishes our anger. If you are feeling awfully triggered because of your backgrounds, ask the Lord to give you a new attitude in your marriage. Allow the Holy Spirit to give you understanding and empathy for your spouse. Would switching to Saturday-night church services instead of going on Sundays, like you did growing up, be a blessing to your wife? Then so be it. Is spending Thanksgiving with your husband's parents very important to his side of the family? Then join in with a happy spirit.

I have one more thought I'd like us to explore biblically. At the risk of sounding dismissive, I'd like to take a look at 1 Corinthians 7:29–31 (NIV). In this passage, Paul urges believers to keep priorities straight:

"What I mean, brothers and sisters, is that the time is short. From now on those who have wives should live as if they do not; those who mourn, as if they did not; those who are happy, as if they were not; those who buy something, as if it were not theirs to keep; those who use the things of the world, as if not engrossed in them. For this world in its present form is passing away."

Paul is teaching that marriage should not at all reduce one's devotion to the Lord and service to Him. The cares of marriage—like how our upbringing shaped us or the customs we hold—are secondary to our spiritual growth. Learning to adjust, compromise, and live selflessly with our husbands and wives is a vehicle for becoming more like Christ. Is that "thing" you keep arguing over really all that important? Can you let some of your attachments to things or ideas go?

Marriage should refine us. Purify us. Make us better. Our differences should serve to expand our hearts and open our minds. Instead, our differences often trigger us and seek to tear us apart. Recently, a business associate who was helping us navigate a contract remarked, "A good settlement is when nobody is happy."[28] I didn't like the sound of that. A marriage contract should never have such a dismal perspective, and yet many of us would describe our marriages as places where "nobody is happy." The only saving grace is having gentle and biblical responses to these triggers. Making our spouse happy isn't our job, but it should be our delight. God has a good plan for every marriage if we are open to new things. Responding with gentleness and an optimistic attitude toward change isn't just about compromise. It's about living lives that complement one another, and that is a tradition worth keeping.

> *Making our spouse happy isn't our job, but it should be our delight.*

Let's Pray: "Lord, I know that my past upbringing has shaped me, just my spouse's upbringing has shaped him/her. Jesus, help us to take the best things from our pasts and use them to make something new in our own marriage. Cleanse us from wrong thinking and attitudes. Help us to appreciate our differences and to be excited about how You have brought us together to be a blessing to one another. Jesus, forgive me for being self-centered. Change me! Let me see my spouse in a new light that expands my capacity for loving-kindness. Don't let our triggers tempt us into angry arguments. Let us see them as opportunities to grow together. We can't change the past, but we trust that You will help us to make the most of our future together. In Jesus' Name, Amen!"

CHAPTER 27

WHEN YOUR FAMILY NEEDS YOU BUT YOU WANT ALONE TIME (GUY)

The stand-up comedian Jeff Allen once told a funny story about a time he made the right decision early in his marriage: "You have to learn how your spouse communicates. It took me two years to figure out that my wife Tami will never tell me to do anything around the house; if she wants me to do something, she will ask me a question; it is from that question that I have to stand there and figure out what she wants me to do.

"My favorite question was when we were newlyweds—I was leaving the house with golf clubs on my shoulder, golf shoes in my hand, and every married person in America knows what she asked me . . . 'Where you going?' I was only married a couple of months. I didn't know the rules. I said, 'I'm going bowling, Columbo!' If you are a newlywed taking notes, that would be the wrong answer. Two hours later, I was still in the living room. 'What is this about, Sweetheart? I can still make the back nine!'

"It's about the right answer, knowing why your beautiful, intelligent wife would ask such a banal question. I know better today; today, if I am leaving the house with golf clubs on my shoulder and golf shoes in my hand and she asks where I'm going, I say, 'I am going to put these in the trunk and then I am going to mow the lawn. I was just practicing leaving for golf . . .'"[29] That Jeff Allen is a smart man.

Family life is rarely one of leisure, particularly for couples with young children. One of the most harmful triggers for couples is the inequity of responsibilities and the general pressures of meeting the needs of others while also keeping yourself fed, inspired, and rejuvenated. Still, Jesus gives us an example of setting aside time to rest and replenish, as well as a picture of what sacrificial love and service looks like. Couples who can work together to find balance ultimately create homes where resentment gives way to peace. It's not wrong to yearn for a break or engage in self-care. Both men and women desire a little time to get away from the demands of family and reconnect with personal interests, even the smallest escape for a quick walk with a friend, a trip to the local coffeehouse, or a hot bath at home without someone banging on the door asking for snacks. Any of those breaks can go a long way in renewing the soul. This desire for alone time away from the constant needs of our families is not a bad thing, but when it's misused or abused, it can be a stumbling block in marriage. Unaddressed, feelings of frustration fester quickly, becoming an explosive trigger to anger and disconnection. The biggest triggers occur when the scales don't seem balanced. One spouse or the other is more committed to their need for leisure than their commitment to being sensitive to the needs of their spouse or kids.

As Amber and I prepared to write this book, we got feedback from friends and readers about this particular trigger. In the middle of our research, Amber and I both started to notice a trend that became troubling. Amber got many responses from women expressing their frustration with their husbands' use of gaming. The pull to tune out while playing video games was so widespread that we knew we needed to address it here.

We understand the desire to sit, turn off your brain, and launch into a fantasy world of gaming. As a father of four boys, I often see the joy and fun this brings. But I also see the addiction. If you're coming home from work after a long day away from your family and the first thing you do is kick off your shoes and have a little of your own time to play video games, or if you steal away after the kids' bedtime to go online instead of using that time to connect with your wife, I'm letting you know that you're missing out on the amazing blessings that the Lord has in store for you in your relationships.

1 Corinthians 13:11 (KJV) says, "When I was a child, I spoke as a child, I understood as a child, I thought as a child; but when I became a man, I put away childish things . . ."

It's not a bad thing to set aside time for gaming once in a while, but when that desire is daily and it becomes more important than spending time with your children or your wife or even giving your wife a break when she's been home with the kids all day, you are not serving your family well or living out your calling. We often fail to see the value in communication, and communication is the key to setting healthy expectations for both husband and wife. If you are turning to video games to find relief from your day, you are turning to the wrong thing. Both your spouse and your God are much better choices.

In recent years, Amber and I have realized that life is short. We want to make the most of it, and we recognize that when we have an eternal perspective, we are reminded that we have only so much time to make an impact for God's Kingdom here on Earth.

The first portion of Isaiah 61 gives us worthy ways to spend our time. It's a commission we can take to heart: to encourage the poor, to help the brokenhearted, to decree the release of captives, to console those who mourn, to strengthen others, and to declare the freedom we have in Christ.

God has given all of us a charge to bless others, help orphans and widows, and minister to prisoners. If we have children, God expects us to be mindful of the best ways to teach and train our kids, recognizing their unique needs and pace of development. That takes intentional planning. God calls us to spread the gospel, help our neighbors, and do our work heartily as unto the Lord. If we are honest, I bet a lot of us waste much precious time on meaningless activities. I know I do! Perhaps it's time to consider the way we use our time, making the most of every opportunity, knowing that when eternity comes, we won't want to look back at how much time we devoted to things that don't have any real value.

Still, that's not to say we can't take time to be refreshed. Mark 1:35, NIV, shows us Jesus' example: "Very early in the morning, while it was still dark, Jesus got up, left the house and went off to a solitary place, where he prayed."

Jesus himself had a deep desire, from time to time, to escape the responsibilities of those who followed Him, and He often stole away to rejuvenate His spirit, connect with His Father, and spend time in prayer for the people and for His ministry. Jesus was known to cross a river to get to the other side to find solace (John 10:39–41, NIV). When He needed to find a quiet place to pray, He would wake early in the morning and go for a walk

(Luke 5:16, NIV). He paddled out onto the water in a boat to get some time to himself (Matthew 14:13, NIV) and even scurried up a mountainside (Matthew 14:23, NIV). Jesus spent a lot of time by lakes and rivers, praying and stealing away time for Himself to process and prepare. And yet, even these efforts to find alone time were thwarted by the crowds that followed Him. Jesus did not paddle away in anger or frustration from the crowd. He sought for Himself some space, but then He turned and spoke with them from the boat, giving of himself, yet again. He always put the needs of others before His own and He did so from a place of compassion. He is our example.

In my own marriage, I didn't start out with this understanding, that's for sure. Those first few months of marriage, while embracing the new me, I will admit I was challenged from day one. After years and years of dedication and sacrifice to my job, twelve-to-fourteen-hour days at work, and then four more hours at home reading scripts and watching tapes, proving my work ethic, building my career, taking business lunches and dinners to build my connections, and more, I had to change my habits. I gladly dropped it all so that I could come home ready to relax and recharge with my beautiful new bride, ready to share evenings with her cooking and watching TV, then snuggling on the couch. But after a few months, those old instincts kicked in and I began to fall back into old work habits, especially as I witnessed colleagues climbing the ladder around me. The stress and reality of my conundrum became another trigger in my marriage, and I struggled with how to split my time between my work and my wife. Worse, I struggled with how to communicate this to my bride, who was a high-school English literature teacher, home by 3:00 P.M. every day. Even though she was pursuing her master's degree while teaching full-time, she was generally done with her work well before I came home from mine. She looked forward to being with me, and I didn't take it to heart. Many angry and tearful arguments resulted.

Within months of our wedding, we found ourselves expecting a child and on the threshold of a whole new version of marriage before we had even gotten the first stage right. I began staying up late after my depleted and very pregnant bride went to bed. Work became a convenient excuse to have "me time." When Amber would express her desire for me to come to bed with her every night, I relented and gave in a few nights, eventually working my way back out to the living room. It wasn't that I didn't want to be with her; I just had this strong need for downtime, *my* time. Amber was frustrated, I was frustrated, and that trigger festered, causing damage to our marriage that took years to overcome. That was the foundation of our then nascent marriage, and once the baby came along, we moved blindly into parenting. I remember using my son's inability to sleep through the night—he had intense colic and acid reflux—as an opportunity to watch live matches of the 2007 Rugby World Cup at 3:00 A.M. while rocking him in the living room, even though he was finally asleep! I should have put him down in his crib and joined my wife. I was that desperate, I was that blind, and in my ignorance I was missing out on the best friend I could ever ask for.

It literally took me years to figure this out, but once I did, I saw an incredible change in my marriage, in the joy of my sons and the love of my wife. Not only that, but my faith has been recharged. It took a career change and a lifestyle change to refocus my sights on what was most important in my life.

The key to this trigger is finding balance between time for yourself and time for your family. That said, love is sacrificial. Even if we never have time for ourselves, we don't have to feel stressed and on edge. Our attitudes and willingness to meet the needs of others will never be a loss if we do it unto the Lord. If your leisure time is a problem for your spouse, it's a problem for you. Our husbands and wives should never question where our devotion lies. Ask the Lord to make you a joyful giver—joyful in giving your time, joyful in giving of yourself—and you will find that the refreshment you seek is not always found in relaxing alone, but in being together.

> *If your leisure time is a problem for your spouse, it's a problem for you.*

Let's Pray: "Lord, thank You for my spouse, my children, and my friendships. I pray, Lord, that You will constantly be my example of how to spend my time well and when there are moments where I feel the anger and frustration rising about my lack of personal time, I pray You would remind me of the gifts I have been entrusted with and that You would replenish my soul in ways that give life to my husband/wife. As I pour myself out, I believe that You will fill me up! Life is short, Lord. I don't want to have any regrets about how I spent my time. Give me and my spouse creative ways to connect and help him/her to know that he/she can always count on me—that nothing is more important to me than my spouse's needs. In Jesus' Name, Amen!"

CHAPTER 28

WHEN YOU DON'T FEEL LOVED (AMBER)

*A*s a former literature teacher, I've had my fair share of reading love stories. History and literature are replete with legendary tales of romance and marital love, from Romeo and Juliet to modern-day Prince Harry and Meghan Markle. Romance novels comprised nearly one-third—29 percent—of the 2015 fiction market. In 2013, romance novel sales exceeded $1 billion, according to Romance Writers of America. And it's not just women reading them. Men make up a respectable 16 percent of romance readers.[30] The Hallmark Channel continues to thrive, airing romance movies every day, all day. As a culture, we are hungry for happy endings off-screen and beyond the book, so we escape into the world of scripted scenes, imagining what could be. But when our own relationships fall short, we get angry and resentful.

Gary Chapman famously changed the vernacular of Christian marriage when he wrote *The 5 Love Languages*. Many couples are familiar with the varying styles, like words of affirmation or gift giving, which are ways individuals offer and receive messages of love. But what if you communicate your desire for a more loving relationship and your husband doesn't get it? Or your wife hears you loud and clear, but it becomes head knowledge that never really translates to the heart? What if your husband knows what you need but doesn't bother to offer it to you? If ignorance is no longer the issue, how do we deal with the anger and resentment of feeling unloved? And how can we honor God when our hearts are hurting?

The saddest conversations I have with readers are with those who feel unloved by their husbands or wives. Without love, we cope under conditions that God never intended. Couples become roommates, or worse. I hear from readers who are at the lowest points in their marriages. Sometimes, they tell me that they aren't sure life is worth living. They are desperate to be heard, agonizing over the arguments they have with their spouses. Even the very presence of their husband or wife in the room rankles them. The coldness of these relationships can lead to divorce if not dealt with.

In my own marriage, I have felt this torment. I had to stop the madness, *literally.* Being mad at my husband robbed me of my joy and crushed my spirit. I had to choose to focus on myself, knowing that I could not change Guy. Most of my readers who find themselves in this painful place tell me that leaving is not an option because they want to keep their family together. Maybe you can identify with that? I encourage you to take off the boxing gloves and yield your spouse to God in prayer. Personally, I committed to examining what God says about love in the Bible and I discovered that my ideas about love were misguided. Feelings of love were absent, and so I believed that my marriage was hopeless. Instead, I realized that love is an *attitude*. Warm romantic feelings come after true biblical love is put into action. Each day, I took a verse about love and chose to live it out practically toward my husband.

Our relationship took a sharp turn. It took time, but when one person loves another like Jesus does, it's nearly impossible for that other person to remain unchanged. We must stop fighting our husbands and wives and start fighting the real enemy, Satan. He wants us to nag, ignore, bristle, and withdraw. We fight against that by doing the exact opposite. When we show unconditional love to our husbands and wives, we disarm the forces of evil hell-bent on destroying our marriages. We can't wait for our spouses to make us feel loved. We must take the initiative. That sounds a lot like Someone else I know:

We must stop fighting our husbands and wives and start fighting the real enemy, Satan.

"We love because he first loved us." (I John 4:19, NIV)

Jesus loved us first. We talked about having a "Me First Attitude" in chapter 22. When we live this out, we will have healthy marriages to show for it. God's Word is not an empty dialogue; it's an active instruction manual for our everyday lives. Here's how we can apply it regarding demonstrations of love in our marriages:

"Let all that you do be done in love." (1 Corinthians 16:14, ESV) Take out the trash, in love. Compliment her dress, in love. Give him a kiss, in love. Call her on your lunch break, in love. Tell him you appreciate his hard work, in love. Approach your financial problem, in love. Invite her into the bedroom, make him his favorite meal, clean up another mess, settle the kids' arguing, *in love*. Do *everything* from a place of love, being filled by the Holy Spirit, whether or not your spouse does the same.

"A new commandment I give to you, that you love one another: just as I have loved you, you also are to love one another. By this all people will know that you are my disciples, if you have love for one another." (John 13:34–35, ESV)

When she nags you, love her like Jesus loves you. When he doesn't help with the kids enough, love him like Jesus does. If she takes you for granted, love her like Jesus. If he hurts your feelings, love him like Jesus. And by so doing, you will accomplish something eternal, being an example and a testimony to your kids and to those in your world who are watching what it's like to be a Christ-follower. Loving our spouses like Jesus may be the greatest commission you or I will ever do. Regrets will be a thing of the past in Heaven, but I imagine we will wish we had not wasted our time being angry about what we did or did not receive from our spouses while we were on Earth. We will simply wish we had loved like Jesus did.

"And above all these put on love, which binds everything together in perfect harmony." (Colossians 3:14, ESV)

In addition to having compassion, kindness, humility, gentleness, and patience, trade anger and bitterness for love. Wouldn't it be amazing to describe your marriage as one of "perfect harmony"? When he leaves the dishwasher loaded, put on humility with love. When she tries to tell you how to drive, put on compassion with love. Don't ever underestimate God's instructions. Living out Colossians 3:14 time and time again will not deplete you. It will replace the tumult of your frustrations with purpose and hope.

"Above all, keep loving one another earnestly, since love covers a multitude of sins." (1 Peter 4:8, ESV)

When he sins, keep loving your husband, earnestly. When she sins, keep loving your wife, earnestly. Love is a holy equalizer, removing the record of wrongs from our memories. You and I both have committed a multitude of wrongs ourselves. We can keep track, or we can keep our marriages intact.

Author Gary Chapman gives a personal example of this. When he felt like his wife was not being loving toward him:

> "I asked my wife three questions:
> 1) What can I do to help you?
> 2) How can I make your life easier?
> 3) How can I be a better husband to you?
>
> Her answers led my behavior. When I started serving her as Christ served His disciples, her attitude toward me changed."[31]

For Chapman, God changed his attitude through prayer as he actively chose to love his wife like Christ. The same can transpire in our hearts. Acts of love create a breeding ground for feelings to germinate. Any reasonable spouse will respond to being loved well. Loving your husband breaks down his defenses. Loving your wife softens her spirit. Biblical marital love begins with obedience and ends with blessing upon blessing.

The Message version of 1 Corinthians 13:4–10 puts things plainly for us: "If I give everything I own to the poor and even go to the stake

Love is a holy equalizer, removing the record of wrongs from our memories. You and I both have committed a multitude of wrongs ourselves. We can keep track, or we can keep our marriages intact.

to be burned as a martyr, but I don't love, I've gotten nowhere. So, no matter what I say, what I believe, and what I do, I'm bankrupt without love.

> Love never gives up.
> Love cares more for others than for self.
> Love doesn't want what it doesn't have.
> Love doesn't strut,
> Doesn't have a swelled head,
> Doesn't force itself on others,
> Isn't always 'me first,'
> Doesn't fly off the handle,
> Doesn't keep score of the sins of others,
> Doesn't revel when others grovel,
> Takes pleasure in the flowering of truth,
> Puts up with anything
> Trusts God always,
> Always looks for the best,
> Never looks back,
> But keeps going to the end."

If you love your spouse, you will actively look for ways to enhance his/her life on a daily basis. Does that describe *you*? I've been in your shoes, brokenhearted friend. I know what it's like to feel desperate in my need for affection. Like so many of my readers, I have been in a place of constant bickering and I've been in a place of cold indifference in my marriage. Neither of those conditions is worth settling for. God as-

Acts of love create a breeding ground for feelings to germinate.

sures us that love is the answer, and while it's wonderful to be on the receiving end, God instructs us to be His conduit, first and foremost. God always equips us to do what He asks of us. It's doable if you're available. Do you want to feel love in your marriage? Nothing will fill your heart more than mirroring the unconditional love of Christ toward your spouse. Love with everything you've got, and you'll have everything to gain.

> *God always equips us to do what He asks of us.*

Let's Pray: "Jesus, thank You for loving me. When I consider how much You have loved me, even at my worst, I am humbled. I know that I can't manufacture loving feelings, but I believe Your Word is truth. I believe that if I am obedient, love will flourish in my marriage. Help us to not fly off the handle! Stop us from keeping a record of wrongs. Help us to always look for the best in one another! Lord, it hurts when I don't feel loved by my spouse, but I refuse to give in to hopelessness. Jesus, I can picture our relationship as one where love cannot be contained. You promise that You can do things beyond all we ask or imagine . . . Thank You for being a God of hope! In Jesus' Name, Amen!"

CHAPTER 29

WHEN PAST WOUNDS SURFACE (AMBER)

Benjamin Franklin said, "Guests, like fish, smell after three days." In other words, don't wear out your welcome. Unfortunately, old wounds have a way of taking up residence in our homes, hindering intimacy, sabotaging connections, and stirring up anger. These unwelcome guests do more than just stink—they disrupt, disjoint, and divide couples from experiencing all God designed for marriage.

How do you know if your past wounds are at play when you are triggered by anger? Experts say that whenever there is chronic fighting in a relationship, it's likely that pain from our past is fueling the flame. Sometimes, we aren't even aware this is happening, but present-day conflicts trigger old memories that bring up feelings of pain, fear, or mistrust. If we fail to recognize that pain from our past is causing some of our marriage triggers, then we can't always move forward into a better relationship.

Psychologist Karen Young tells readers to identify the cause of their anger by asking these three questions:

1. Is the conflict constant? Does it always feel the same?
2. Is your emotional reaction to whatever is triggering your anger and frustration out of proportion to whatever seemed to cause it? Does your spouse often tell you that you are overreacting?
3. Do you get stuck, unable to shift your reaction, time and time again?[32]

If you are nodding your head here, then most likely, some of the anger you are experiencing has roots in the past.

Two key gentle biblical responses are helpful for those of us who find ourselves with these kinds of anger issues. The first is to trade angry reactions like yelling, withdrawing from one another, or quarreling for a commitment to turn to the Lord for healing. The second biblical response is to extend empathy to our hurting spouses. Showing compassion is far better than matching their frustrations with our own.

FINDING HEALING

Recently, my friend Janet slumped onto my couch as I handed her a cup of hot tea. Silent tears began to fall as she struggled to speak. "I know the insecurities from my past haven't healed. But the hardest part is that I really believed my husband would see my weakness and help me get over it. I thought my marriage would be the place that I would finally feel whole."

Janet had been married for a while, but the conflicts in her marriage were worsening. After bickering for the past year, the weight was taking its toll. She felt doomed to a future of angst and discord.

Whether you are the spouse who *has* past wounds that are affecting your relationship or you are *married to* someone who needs healing from childhood trauma or other broken relationships, there is always hope for the Christ-follower. Because God's Word is true, we can take Psalm 147:3 (ESV) to heart: "He heals the brokenhearted and binds up their wounds." Remember, triggers are opportunities for growth! This trigger may be a blessing in disguise, forcing you or your spouse to finally let the walls down, allowing the Holy Spirit to bind up wounds and strengthen your marriage. That's the first step toward responding in a way that honors God. I know it's painful to revisit the disappointments, losses, and harm that have come to us over the course of our lives, but an honest look back, prayerfully considering where we may need healing, is imperative.

Jesus went to great lengths to heal our hearts, as we see in 1 Peter 2:24 (ESV): "He himself bore our sins in his body on the tree, that we might die to sin and live to righteousness. By his wounds you have been healed." I love that Jesus declares to us that we "have been healed" in the past tense. We sometimes get in the way of our own healing if we don't own what Jesus did for us on the cross.

The apostle Peter had plenty of failures and challenges that could have crippled him. He nearly drowned when his faith faltered while walking on water. And it was Peter who denied even knowing Jesus as His dear Friend was being led to the cross. Peter endured persecution and hardship. Instead of walking wounded, he took to heart what Jesus had done for him, and in so doing he moved forward as a godly and influential leader in the early church. Peter's name in Greek is Petros, which means "rock." It's hard to do damage to a rock, isn't it? Rocks are solid and stable, useful and strong. Rocks withstand a lot of pressure. Your name may not mean "rock," but your Jesus is the rock and foundation on which you stand. He steadies our hearts and emotions, our great Healer who helps us overcome our pasts.

It's no coincidence that in the same chapter in the book of Ephesians where marital love is described, God gives us the formula for hearts to be made whole:

"For husbands, this means love your wives, just as Christ loved the church. He gave up his life for her to make her holy and clean, washed by the cleansing of God's word. He did this to present her to himself as a glorious church without a spot or wrinkle or any other blemish. Instead, she will be holy and without fault." (Ephesians 5:25–27, NLT)

It is being "washed by the cleansing of God's word" that makes any of us holy and clean. Jesus presents His Bride, which is the Body of believers, "without spot or wrinkle." The guilt of our sinfulness is removed in God's eyes. If He can purify our hearts from unrighteousness, then He is also able to purify us from the negative impact of events that happened to us before we were married. It's true that past wounds leave scars. But our scars are not the wounds themselves. They are simply evidence that we have survived. God's Word cleanses us from sinful patterns so that we never have to engage in the same old arguments. Guy and I want to emphasize that some of these deeper issues are best discussed under the discerning eye of a professional counselor or pastor who can help clear some of the cobwebs and help you process the pain

> *It's true that past wounds leave scars. But our scars are not the wounds themselves. They are simply evidence that we have survived.*

and receive God's healing. That said, we are able, through the Holy Spirit, to offer gentle and biblical responses, even when past wounds surface.

EXTENDING EMPATHY TO HURTING SPOUSES

In the middle of some of our worst arguments, I have tearfully asked Guy these questions:

Even if I'm terribly wrong here, could you love me like I'm not?
If my tone is angry or offensive, could you be gentle and kind?
If I'm being impatient, could you show me patience?
If I'm being unreasonable, can you be reasonable with me?

In my childhood, there was very little grace—giving me what I did not deserve. Many times, I wasn't even sure why I was in trouble. Little things were met with swift punishments. So even when I am sinful or in error, to have someone show me gracious love is an opportunity for Guy to assist in my healing. Having a husband who would see my faults and treat me with loving-kindness, instead of matching my ugliness, was crucial for my well-being. I had never experienced that in any earthly relationship. I longed for a husband who would begin to show me that aspect of God's character played out in real life.

When our husbands and wives' past wounds invade our marriage, it's a chance for us to live out the grace of God toward them. Of all the blessings of marriage, one of the greatest is the opportunity to be the hands and feet of Jesus to another human being. What a missed opportunity if we waste it being angry and unsympathetic, or closed off to our own healing! It requires a shift in our views about our spouse's past wounds. Instead of seeing them as problems to fix or avoid, it's an opportunity to love another human being in the way that Jesus loves *us*.

It's easy to filter what our spouses say through our upbringing. For years, I'd say something to Guy and he heard "You're stupid" or "You messed that up." When we went back over the conversation, he finally realized that what I said was not what he heard. The wounds from his past spoke lies to him. Talking through our conversations out loud brings them into the light and gives us an opportunity to remove harmful filters that Satan can use to create discord. Guy and I were both willing to calmly address these misperceptions, pray over those old wounds, and communicate in ways that released us from this trigger.

When you become embroiled in the same war of words over and over again, it's a good practice to stop and repeat to your spouse what you think you are hearing for clarification. Guy and I have been surprised by how often we have misread or misheard one another because the filter we are using is damaged by our past wounds. If our filter is inaccurate, we won't see clearly, communicate effectively, or have the tools we need to move in an untriggered direction. Taking the time to listen and then both *confirm and affirm* what your spouse is saying alleviates a lot of miscommunication.

Empathic spouses seek to understand and share in the feelings of their husband or wife. In Romans 12:15 (ESV), the apostle Paul instructs us, "Rejoice with those who rejoice, weep with those who weep." Who better to experience this with than the one we promised to love and cherish?

Empathy responds gently instead of getting exasperated when your husband's ego is wounded. It doesn't say, "I told you so" when he messes up, further wounding his sense of self. Instead, empathy says, "That must be discouraging. I'm sorry you are experiencing this." Empathy doesn't say, "Why must you always cry?" when your wife's reaction to conflict is emotional. Instead, it puts its arm around her, comfortingly. Empathy says, "Your tears show me how deeply this is bothering you. I'm here for you." Empathy doesn't dismiss situations that are important to your wife or husband even if they're not important to you. We value what our spouse values because we value our spouse. Empathy desires to understand, instead of fix. And it seeks to connect, instead of pulling away. Empathetic husbands and wives feel their heart soften in triggered moments, instead of allowing their blood to boil. Empathy embodies Luke 6:31 (NIV), "Do to others as you would have them do to you." The familiar saying "Life is a journey, not a destination" is fitting when we talk about marriage. Most of us promised "till death us do part." That may be a very long journey, indeed! When I reach the end of my days, I don't want to look back with regret. A few years ago, I had a serious health scare. I wasn't sure if the doctors were going to give me a diagnosis that would result in my life being cut short. I'm incredibly thankful that test results came back without any concerns, but it gave me a couple of weeks to reevaluate much about my life. When you think you may be reaching the end of your days on Earth, perspectives come into sharp focus. All I wanted to do was make things right in my relationships. I wanted to say "yes" more often to my kids. I longed to have meaningful conversations with my friends. And I was purposeful to be much more in tune with the needs of my husband, seeking to let

We value what our spouse values because we value our spouse.

all the "little things" go that suddenly didn't matter very much. The past, and all my wounds, paled in comparison to my desire to live in the moment. I haven't forgotten that feeling.

For some couples, shifting from feeling triggered by past wounds to becoming vulnerable to the healing process may very well be the most important spiritual discipline they will ever face. Some couples have chosen to give up. They remain stagnant or, worse, volatile. That kind of negative energy depletes our joy. While facing these challenges is not easy, it's worse to remain angry. Choosing to stay in the game and walk through past wounds with our spouses is worth the hard work and refinement we will face. That's what love does. And in the end, our marriages will fulfill God's purpose for our lives, transforming us into selfless men and women with hearts made whole.

Let's Pray: "Heavenly Father, You are our Healer. My brokenness is not too broken for You to restore. Lord, it feels overwhelming to lay down my anger in exchange for gentle biblical responses. Instead, I want You to overwhelm me with Your peace. Heal my hurting heart, Lord! Take the pain and turn it into something beautiful. Open my eyes to seeing how this trigger impacts my spouse. Give us both the desire to walk this road together, seeking to show empathy and love. Lord, restore our wasted years of bickering, caught in an angry cycle. We invite You in to heal and redeem our marriage. Make our hearts clean and without spot, by the washing of Your mighty Word! In Jesus' Name, Amen!"

CHAPTER 30

WHEN YOUR FEELINGS ARE HURT (GUY)

I still remember the day as if it were yesterday. My then fiancée, Amber, and I went to a department store in the heart of Hollywood to register for our wedding gifts. While it's probably more common for women to drive that effort, I am the kind of guy that loves to decorate and shop for the house. My apartment was a 1940s-style four-plex in an old neighborhood of LA with lots of style and personality. The house had arched hallways, beat-up hardwood floors, a stone fireplace, and little cutouts in the walls for candles and books. My roommate and I even had a wall of swords—an entire wall with a pinwheeled display of authentic and stage swords from across the seventeenth and eighteenth centuries, which he collected. We decked the place out with an Italian cottage–style flair. This was no typical bachelor pad.

I enjoyed decorating the home nicely, buying great cookware, and having the "perfect" coffee cups, just like the next guy. Naturally, I wanted a say in what kind of plates I was going to be eating from for the next twenty years and even which toaster I was going to be using in the kitchen. Understandably, Amber had envisioned this to be her deal and that I was just there to appreciate her style. My wife is an extreme planner and visionary, and she is also one of the most efficient people I have ever met, so naturally she had been dreaming about this life stage since she was a child—the colors and location of her wedding, decorating her home and setting things up exactly how she wanted them, so she could use her incredible gift for hospitality to its fullest.

We pulled into the parking lot of Macy's department store. There we sat in the car waiting for the store to open, already in conflict and feeling angry. Amber felt like I was going to rain on her parade, and I felt offended that she didn't want my voice in the matter. After the stalemate and a sudden silence, we both walked into the store, hands at our sides, an unhealthy distance between us. We got our wedding registry "stun guns" from the associate, one for her and one for me, and off we went to enter battle over everyday china and the perfect toaster, each of us in an angry huff.

As we stood in front of the wall of casual china, Amber said as if prepared for an argument, "I like that one with the Italian pines on the rim!" Shaking my head up and down slowly and perusing the wall one extra time for added dramatic effect, I stated, "Well, I like that one with the Italian pine trees on the rim as well!" (So there!) Row by row, we moved on to the next item on our wish list. We came to the water glasses, and lo and behold, after a moment of careful consideration we both revealed our choices, expecting to disagree. *But we didn't.* To my surprise as well as hers, we once again agreed. Then the formal china, same thing. We both started to relax a bit and the tension began to dissipate, our fingers slowly lessening the pressure on the triggers on our guns and the triggers in our hearts. By the time we got to the silverware, we realized we were in fact on the exact same page about nearly everything! We began to laugh. I am pretty sure I got a kiss on the way out.

This was a defining event in our lives as Amber and I found ourselves on the same page even when we thought we were so far off. Our initial anger and lack of loving communication had forced us both to act like fools, almost ruining what became a memorable moment in our story. We were still learning about each other, but one of our first lessons was to not jump to conclusions. Ecclesiastes 7:9 (NIV) says, "Do not be quickly provoked in your spirit, for anger resides in the lap of fools." We were feeling foolish, alright.

Not every time we hurt one another's feelings turns out so well. Over the years, we have learned a few important tactics to prevent and manage the trigger of hurt feelings in our marriage:

Brush a lot of stuff off. Of the two of us, I'm the more sensitive one, believe it or not. It's harder for me to not become defensive, but this is an area of growth where I am learning not to take everything to heart. Ecclesiastes 7:21–22 (ESV) puts it this way:

"Do not take to heart all the things that people say, lest you hear your servant cursing you. Your heart knows that many times you yourself have cursed others."

Convicting, huh? It's wise to guard our hearts from every little comment or action that seeks to wound us. Choose not to let molehills become mountains in your marriage.

Verify before you vilify. For many years in our marriage, Amber and I were quick to vilify one another before verifying what one or the other of us really meant by what we said or did. We talked about this a little bit earlier in the book, but it bears repeating here: Believe the best about each other first. Make sure you are clearly understanding what your spouse was really saying or meaning, and if all else fails, and your spouse truly is in the wrong, evaluate whether you can let it go or if you need to come together to communicate outside of conflict. Remember, Matthew 5:44 tells us to love even our enemies, so even when your spouse is being sinful, you can be loving in the midst of your hurt.

Don't get protective, get proactive. When our feelings are hurt, we often go into protection mode, placing walls around our hearts so that doesn't happen again. That doesn't just become a barrier against pain, it becomes a blockade to intimacy with our spouse. Instead, be proactive to communicate with your spouse, take time to pray and release your hurt to the Lord, and then do something to bless your husband or wife. Not long ago, Amber and our son Quinn had a chance to put this into practice. Amber shared about it on her social media:

"Kids at school said horrible things today. Made me boil. I needed a distraction, so I picked up my keys to head to the grocery store. Quinn asked if he could come. 'Yes,' I said. And as he shared further about his hard day, my heart sank. Pulling into the parking lot, I had an idea. 'Quinn,' I suggested, 'let's turn it around. You can only do you. I can only do me. We can't change those mean things those other kids did to you today. But we can bless some people here tonight. We can be different. Let's serve others and be extra kind. Like lights in the dark. Let's watch for ways to help people.' He eagerly jumped out of the car. We spotted a large, heavy cart tipped upside down in a huge ditch. Quinn yelled, 'Come on, Mom!' He began to lift it. This wasn't quite what I had in mind. My hesitation lasted only a moment and then I joined him. Together, we heaved it up and out and set it next to the other massive carts. We smiled and headed toward the store and as we looked up, an employee headed our way and called out a grateful thank-you, grinning from ear to ear. He'd caught us doing good. My boy bounced happily along, offering a fist bump. That's the best way I know how to put a spring back in his step. It's not in revenge. Or shielding him from pain. It's by reminding us both that we can only do the next right thing, ourselves."

Being proactive with our pain is always better than nursing it. For Christ-followers, it also brings beauty from ashes.

Living in a lost and fallen world, we are positioned for pain, but we are also positioned for hope in the midst of it. Your spouse will hurt your feelings. You will hurt his or hers. Whether or not it leads you to anger is within your power to control. Whenever we experience sorrow or affliction, we are given an opportunity to identify with Christ. God will use it if we don't lose

God will use it if we don't lose it!

it! Know that He looks on you with hopeful expectation that you will respond with the same grace that He so often extends to you.

Let's Pray: "Lord, sometimes I hurt so badly that it blinds me to any hope for connection with my husband/wife. Heal my pain, Lord. Forgive me for the times that I have caused my spouse pain. I don't want us to wound each other anymore. Lord, give us compassion and understanding toward one another. Instead of our being too sensitive, grow us in sensitivity toward one another's feelings. Help me to be discerning about what I can let go and what areas we need to work through together. Father, thank You for opening our eyes to this issue and lead us toward loving-kindness. In Jesus' Name, Amen!"

CHAPTER 31

WHEN YOUR MARRIAGE NEEDS A DO-OVER (AMBER)

The door creaked open as I silently slipped outside. The kids were in bed, and after attempting to hold it all together, I let it out. My anger had given way to discouragement. I sat on the back patio in the cold winter air, holding my even colder heart in my hands, offering it to the Lord, begging Him to revive it.

My marriage was no Cinderella story. After yet another angry encounter with Guy, I just didn't have the strength to try anymore. I simply wanted the pain to stop. That night, years ago now, was a turning point. As I stared out at the evening darkness, the path before me illuminated, giving me clarity about the crossroads I was facing. I had three options. I could continue as I was, lost and hurting, simply trying to keep the peace but aching from my triggered relationship. I could walk away and end my marriage, leaving behind a wake of shattered children and many haunting unknowns. Or I could surrender my heart and my husband to the Lord, determined, one trigger at a time, to begin my own personal do-over. You can guess which choice I made.

Perhaps like me, it is painfully obvious to you as you complete this book that you need a marriage do-over too. Jesus is all about do-overs. Jonah got a do-over. The woman at the well? Do-over. Peter? Him too. King David, Joseph's brothers, Mary Magdalene, Jesus' brother James, Samson, Rahab the prostitute, the Israelites, the repentant thief on the cross, Lazarus, the apostle Paul. So many divine do-overs. If you and your marriage need one too, then join the crowd.

In my book *Parenting Scripts*, I kindly offer this question to my sons when their tone of voice is whiny or rude: "Son, how can you say that differently?" Instead of blowing my top when they forget to be content, respectful, or kind, I am more apt to offer them a "do-over." Reacting with my own angry, whiny, or rude response would be an act of war. My frustration would feed theirs. My short-tempered spirit would inflame theirs. My anger would justify theirs. One of the most life-changing moments in my parenting came when I realized that offering them a chance to try again is what Jesus has done for me, over and over throughout my own spiritual journey. God never whacked me upside the head when I failed. Imagining His face before me, I never saw condemnation there. Gently, lovingly, He beckoned me to a better way. His mercy was new for me, every morning. As I grew in this area of gentle biblical parenting, I recognized that offering my husband—and even myself—a second chance was one of the godliest things I could do for my marriage.

If you've made it this far through *Marriage Triggers*, I'm betting you have a desire for your marriage to be everything God designed it to be. Our prayer is that you have begun to respond instead of reacting, to let go of anger and embrace grace. We hope that you already see the new-ness of your relationship springing forth. For those of us who long for God's best in our marriages, Psalm 84:11 (ESV) offers us an exciting promise: "For the Lord God is a sun and shield; the Lord bestows favor and honor. No good thing does he withhold from those who walk up-rightly."

> *One of the most life-changing moments in my parenting came when I realized that offering them a chance to try again is what Jesus has done for me, over and over throughout my own spiritual journey.*

Satan would have you believe that do-overs are impossible. He wants you to dwell on your triggers and rehearse your hurts. Don't give in to him! Instead, meditate on the hope found in this verse. The Psalmist expresses God's protection over you, His desire to give you both favor and honor, and His commit-ment to give you good things. Do you believe Him? When God made Adam and Eve, joining them together, He called it "good." The Lord does not want you to miss out on the fullness of what your marriage can become and He is willing to help you. Walk uprightly! Your anger has no hold on *you* unless you hold on to *it.* Letting go of our anger frees us to grab hold of the good things God has in store for our marriages. Step into the grace and power of the Holy Spirit to redeem the angry past. Get excited about the love of God and the transforming power of His promises!

As you thumb through these final pages of this book, consider Ephesians 6:12 (NIV): "For our struggle is not against flesh and blood, but against the

> *Your anger has no hold on you unless you hold on to it.*

AMBER LIA & GUY LIA

rulers, against the authorities, against the powers of this dark world and against the spiritual forces of evil in the heavenly realms."

I know your struggle feels like it's against your husband or wife, but it's not. Your marriage feels hard because battles are hard. If you claim to be a Christ-follower and you are married, then like it or not, your marriage is a target for spiritual attack. The devil attacks your marriage via a thousand paper cuts; he doesn't just stab you and get it over with. He shows up to battle with a razor blade full of triggers, but that's no match for the Sword of the Spirit. Strategically, letting go of our anger is how we fight our marriage battles. The war has already been won by Jesus Christ, so we should be acting like victors, not victims. For husbands and wives, do-overs don't mean divorce. Do-overs mean declaring God's mercy, grace, and power over our relationships. Instead of fighting with each other, do-overs give our marriages a fighting chance.

For many years, I have been joining my good friend Angela in praying for her troubled marriage. This past year, everything changed:

"Two years ago, if you had told me that my husband would not only be an amazingly devoted father but a true companion to me, I'd have told you, 'You're off your rocker.' It wasn't until we committed to work on our marriage that everything changed. How? The biggest factor was realizing how families of origin had played a role. I came from a family of 'We'll fix it' and my husband came from a 'Do it yourself' family.

> *The devil attacks your marriage via a thousand paper cuts; he doesn't just stab you and get it over with.*

Add in my codependency and my husband's need for control, and it's no shock we were on the brink of divorce. What made all the difference for us was contracts. That didn't sound so romantic at the time, but neither did divorce papers, so I was more than willing to try. And it

Instead of fighting with each other, do-overs give our marriages a fighting chance.

worked. We wrote out contracts for communication, romance, time, and even how we'd speak to each other. ('I' statements always. No blaming. No shaming. 'Oh, you need a break from this heated conversation, so it doesn't turn into a swirly nightmare? No problem!') I am not going to lie—I burned with anger at my husband for over a year during this process . . . and for a good decade before. But just like I would not abandon my child for having a tantrum, I wasn't willing to abandon my marriage. When I loved on my relationship (not my husband) by giving it the boundaries and safety it needed to heal and thrive, everything changed. If my bitter, self-righteous, resentful, and unforgiving heart could transform through willingness (all rooted in God's love), then anyone's can."

Recently, I received this message from a reader about her marital do-over. Even when Karen was at rock bottom, God was able to bring new life to her relationship:

"After eight years of dating and five years of marriage, I found out my husband had been leading a double life, lying about illegal drug use and keeping his behavior (profanity, risk-taking) a secret from me. I was heartbroken and devastated. I felt like such a fool for having no idea, and angry that I had left my two boys home with him while he was using. I was angry about the risks he took that endangered our entire well-being. The lies felt so heavy. BUT

GOD ... he agreed to counseling and at the first session, he asked Jesus to be his everything! This time, it was genuine. There has been radical transformation, repentance, forgiveness, the rebuilding of trust. There has been backsliding, distrust, and disappointment, too, but the grace of God has covered it all. Things aren't perfect by any means, but I truly believe we are growing closer to God and each other. It's not the road I would have chosen for myself, but God has been so good to both of us!"

Angela's and Karen's words aren't just stories. They are testimonies—examples of God's fulfilled promises to be their Redeemer and to give you hope for your own marriage. And just in case you think that your second chance is strictly about your husband/wife relationship, listen to what my reader Shannon recently shared with me:

"A year into my marriage we were about to divorce. It was awful. We separated because I was having an affair. My husband pursued me, and we decided to try and make it work. Since then our marriage has grown into a strong and good place. We have two special-needs kiddos and one seemingly typical. I think that God gave us the gift of being able to work things out so we could work together for the sake of our children."

The beautiful truth for the Christ-follower is not just that God can use our marriages to bless our own lives, but that our marriages are vehicles for us to bless the lives of others. Shannon and her husband discovered that the strength they gained by conquering their anger and frustration in marriage equipped them to become better, stronger parents. Working together to restore their relationship prepared them to work together as mom and dad to kids who needed their unified efforts in parenting. That's a supernatural bonus!

God is a God of multiplicity. In Christ's economy, everything we do has an impact that multiplies exponentially. Our choices don't merely impact us. They impact everyone in the downline of our influence. When we exchange our angry reactions for gentle biblical responses, we position ourselves as conduits for positively impacting generations of relationships. Luke 1:50 (NIV) says, "His mercy extends to those who fear him, from generation to generation." It's amazing to think that our transformations won't only change our marriages. They have the potential to change the lives of our children and our children's children.

> *The beautiful truth for the Christ-follower is not just that God can use our marriages to bless our own lives, but that our marriages are vehicles for us to bless the lives of others.*

Tomorrow will come, as long as God leaves us here. But don't wait for morning to make a decision to give your triggers to the Lord.

"For he says, 'In the time of my favor I heard you, and in the day of salvation I helped you.' I tell you, now is the time of God's favor, now is the day of salvation." (2 Corinthians 6:2, NIV)

Happiness isn't meant to be the gauge for your commitment to your spouse; it's your commitment to your spouse that will gauge your happiness. And it's your commitment to your God that will make all the difference. There is nothing God can't do in the heart of a child of God. Name your trigger. Name your heartache. If you desire to trade your angry reactions for gentle biblical responses, nothing stands in the way of your transformation. Right here, right now, as you finish reading these final words in this final chapter, make a new vow to your Heavenly Groom. Tell

Him that you are done with feeling irritated, annoyed, enraged, indignant, and exasperated. Tell Him that You are ready to receive His Holy Spirit's power to face every trigger. Tell Him that You will do your part because you know He is always faithful to do His.

Fairy tales get a bad rap, but happily ever after isn't just for make-believe. Just as I held my broken and triggered heart in my hands, offering it to the Lord to revive and restore so many years ago, so you, too, can offer yours. Every trigger is a new opportunity for a do-over. Every response is a choice you make. Your marriage triggers are paving the way for blessings if you resist the temptation to give in to them. Speak calmly instead of yelling. Ask questions instead of making assumptions. Be patient instead of letting your blood boil. Choose to fight the spiritual battle instead of fighting your flesh-and-blood spouse. Yes, dear one, step into all that God designed your marriage to be, releasing your anger and embracing His love. Don't believe for one minute that if you don't have your happy ending, God isn't working. Don't believe that your story is over. Your do-over is your chance for a holy rewrite. Enter into your new beginning and overcome your triggers, one spiritual victory at a time.

Happiness isn't meant to be the gauge for your commitment to your spouse; it's your commitment to your spouse that will gauge your happiness. And it's your commitment to your God that will make all the difference.

Let's Pray: "Dear God, my marriage needs a do-over. I need a do-over! Thank You, Lord, for being a God of mercy who continually gives me another chance to make right choices. I praise You, Lord, for rewriting my marriage story. Thank You for being patient with me, never giving up on me, and promising to be my sun and shield. I want Your favor on my relationship, Lord! I know You won't withhold any good thing from me as I walk uprightly, choosing to respond instead of react. Give us a new beginning and help us to cast away our angry reactions! Father God, we desire gentle biblical responses and we want our relationship to be a testimony of Your ability to make all things new. Thank You, Lord, in advance for reviving my heart, renewing my mind, and showing me the way I should walk. Our story isn't over yet, Lord. I love You, Lord. Here's my heart. Make it Yours. In Jesus' Name, Amen!"

ACKNOWLEDGMENTS

Amber Lia:

Guy, there would be no *Marriage Triggers* without you. No one has ever loved me like you love me. I prayed for my future husband since I was a young girl. I praise God that He answered my prayers by bringing you into my life—my match made in Heaven! We sure were triggered. But we sure are blessed. Thank you for agreeing to write this book with me, but even more so, thank you for living out the godly principles within these pages. I love you, acres and oceans full!

Oliver, Quinn, Oakley, and Quade, you were among the main reasons that your daddy and I fought hard for our marriage. We pray that we can continue to grow into the kind of mom and dad that you will be thankful for. And we hope and pray that our marriage will be an example to you. We have asked the Lord to bless you in your own marriages someday—to bring you wives who will love and respect you and that you will love them as Christ loved the Church. We are so proud of you all! Our hearts are full to overflowing with love for you!

ACKNOWLEDGMENTS

My agent, Janet Grant, nobody works harder on our behalf than you. Thank you for believing in us and our book!

Becky Nesbit, thank you for making us look good. We are so grateful that you championed *Marriage Triggers*! You are a blessing to us.

Guy Lia:

Amber, you are my Forever Bride! Thank you not just for making me a husband and a father but for making me a better husband, a better father, and helping me to become a better, more passionate Christ-follower! Your natural gifts have inspired me and added so much to my life, and I will never be able to express my love for you and for what we have and are creating together. You have checked off all the boxes on my list of requirements and desires for a wife and have caused me to add a bunch of others! With you, I am truly blessed!

Boys, you guys inspire me every day to remember to be more childlike, to get down and play and to live life moment by moment and in the moment. I love you all so very much! Thank you for supporting Mom and Dad during the writing of this wonderful book. You are a part of the story that will hopefully affect thousands of mommies and daddies for the better. With you, I am richly blessed!

Mom and Dad, I am so sorry you could not be here to meet my wife and children and see the fruits of all our labor. I know you are watching from above, and I feel comforted knowing that I have the best life that I can because of you both. Your love has been amazing!

*M*arriage Triggers: Exchanging Spouses' Angry Reactions For Gentle Biblical Responses is a wonderful resource to use as a couple, in small groups, or for church studies. Please visit http://www.motherofknights.com/ for free discussion questions for each chapter of *Marriage Triggers* as well as other books and resources from Amber Lia and Guy Lia.

NOTES

1   Lou Priolo, *The Heart of Anger* (Calvary Press, 1998), Chapter 6.

2   https://me.me/i/funnyparents-and-then-one-day-we-decided-we-were-tired-16828959

3   https://www.inc.com/minda-zetlin/backseat-driver-in-your-car-these-strategies-may-h.html

4   https://www.builtlean.com/2013/09/17/muscles-grow/

5   https://www.desiringgod.org/interviews/what-are-spiritual-disciplines

6   https://www.youtube.com/watch?v=5ODpwqTQky0

7   https://www.amazon.com/Day-Charles-H-Spurgeon/dp/0825437717, p. 65, March 20.

8   https://www.brainyquote.com/quotes/james_dobson_182575

9   Amber Lia & Wendy Speake, *Triggers: Exchanging Parents' Angry Reactions for Gentle Biblical Responses* (Roanoke, Virginia: Same Page Press, 2015), p. 24.

10   Martha Peace, *The Excellent Wife, A Biblical Perspective* (Bemidji, Minnesota: Focus Publishing, Inc., 2005), p. 231.

11   https://tolovehonorandvacuum.com/2012/10/wifey-wednesday-do-not-deprive-roundup/

12   https://www.christianitytoday.com/women/2017/march/god-feminist-ideals-is-bible-good-for-women.html

13   https://tolovehonorandvacuum.com/2013/06/reader-question-husband-spiritual-leader/

14   https://www.psychologytoday.com/us/blog/emotional-fitness/201411
/honesty-can-make-or-break-relationship

15   Luis Palau, *So You Want to Grow* (Irvine, California: Harvest House Publishers, 1986).

16   https://www.webmd.com/balance/guide/causes-of-stress#1-2

17   Luis Palau, *So You Want to Grow* (Irvine, California: Harvest House Publishers, 1986).

18   *NIV Quest Study Bible*, Copyright © 1994, 2003, 2011 by Zondervan.

19   www.goodreads.com/quotes/504650-i-have-a-strange-feeling-with-regard-to-you-as

20   https://jimdaly.focusonthefamily.com/six-predictors-of-marital-success
-and-happiness/

21   Quote by Henry Ford: https://www.brainyquote.com/quotes/henry
_ford_122451

22   Joseph P. Lash, *Helen and Teacher: The Story of Helen Keller and Anne Sullivan Macy* (Delacorte Press/Seymour Lawrence, 1980).

23   Gary Chapman, *The Five Love Languages, How to Express Heartfelt Commitment to Your Mate* (Northfield Publishing, 1995).

24   https://michaelhyatt.com/creating-your-life-plan/

25   Rick Warren, *The Purpose Driven Life* (Grand Rapids, MI: Zondervan, 2002, 2011, 2012) p. 109.

26   https://www.goodreads.com/author/quotes/5139.Charles_R_Swindoll

27   https://skeptics.stackexchange.com/questions/19027/did-socrates-say
-the-secret-of-change-is?rq=1

28   http://www.milesmediation.com/blog/good-settlement-nobody-happy
-right-wrong/

29   https://www.jeffallencomedy.com/

30   https://www.bustle.com/articles/166802-who-reads-romance-novels
-this-infographic-has-the-answer

31   https://www.focusonthefamily.com/marriage/how-to-truly-love
-your-spouse

32   https://www.heysigmund.com/how-to-stop-old-wounds-from-stealing
-into-relationships